DOSSIER 03

PLANNING AND CONTROLLING PROJECTS

The Universal Manager

ACKNOWLEDGEMENTS

This publication was developed by Scitech Educational in partnership with NEBS Management.

Project management:	Diana Thomas (NEBS Management)
	Don McLeod (Scitech Educational)
Series editor:	Darren O'Conor
Authors:	William Aitken, Darren O'Conor

Dossier 03: Planning and Controlling Projects

A Scitech Educational publication

Distributed by Scitech-DIOL

ISBN 0 948672 67 6

Published by:
Scitech Educational Ltd
15 – 17 The St John Business Centre
St Peter's Road
Margate
Kent CT9 1TE
Tel: +44 (0)1843 231494
Fax: +44 (0)1843 231485
Website: www.universal-manager.co.uk
           http://www.scitechdiol.co.uk

CONTENTS

PLANNING AND CONTROLLING PROJECTS

THE UNIVERSAL MANAGER SERIES

Books

01   **Risk Management**
02   **Delivering Successful Projects**
03   **Planning and Controlling Projects**
04   **The Learning Organization**
05   **Managing for Knowledge**
06   **Obtaining and Retaining Customers**
07   **Human Resource Planning**
08   **Business Planning**
09   **Financial Performance**
10   **Managing Quality**
11   **Business Relationships**
12   **Managing for High Performance**
13   **Managing Harmoniously**
14   **21st Century Communication**
15   **Managing for Sustainability**

Computer-based Resources

Management Assignments (CD-ROM)
Personal Developing Planning Toolkit
         (at www.universal-manager.co.uk)
Learning Styles Toolkit
         (at www.universal-manager.co.uk)

PREFACE

Today, the concept of project management enjoys greater visibility and credibility than ever before. The tools and techniques of the discipline have spread far beyond the industry sectors that developed them, and are now just as likely to be employed within a bank or hospital as in a construction or manufacturing company. Project management textbooks and software packages are available in abundance, and there is no shortage of training and consultancy for organizations and individuals who want to learn how it should be done.

There is however a downside to this increasing awareness and buy-in to project management principles. Every sector, every textbook and every software programme seems to have its own unique take on project management — divergence can be found even on fundamental matters such as the definition of key terms (project, programme, design, build, etc.). Round up half a dozen project managers from different backgrounds, leave them to talk for a few minutes, and before long you will have utter confusion. It is not simply that terminologies vary. Even more problematic is that project managers tend to 'specialize' in what they consider to be the essential aspect of project management — for most this is planning, but many focus on the front end definition of a project before detailed planning begins, while others may concentrate on the political realm (relationship building, maintaining a high profile, and so on).

The Universal Manager series attempts to take a balanced view of the total discipline in two dossiers:

- 02   Delivering Successful Projects
- 03   Planning and Controlling Projects.

This dossier, *Planning and Controlling Projects*, examines the 'harder' skills which come into play after project start-up: contracting; planning and scheduling; monitoring, review and evaluation. Key techniques discussed here include the Critical Path Method, resource allocation, earned value analysis and various financial evaluation tests.

Its companion, *Delivering Successful Projects*, concentrates on what might be considered the 'softer' project management skills: initiating and scoping projects, establishing feasibility, building the project team and dealing with the key players.

It also explores the evolution of project management theory from post-war US Department of Defence developments, to the more recent concepts of 'lean thinking' and 'modified design'.

Overall, we hope that both dossiers provide a clear and even-handed view of the theories, processes, tools and techniques which together make up project management. The material in both has been designed for study by practising and aspiring project managers, with an emphasis on encouraging the transfer of learning to the workplace.

As well as providing a wealth of information for the general reader, *Planning and Controlling Projects* will support candidates working towards the NEBS Management Diploma and the Management S/NVQ at Level 4.

If you are working towards either qualification, your approved centre will provide guidance on how your study of *Planning and Controlling Projects* fits in with the overall programme. Appendix 3 of this dossier contains information about the NEBS Management Diploma.

LEARNING PROFILE

Topics included in this dossier are listed below. Use them to make a quick judgement about the level of your current knowledge and understanding, and to highlight the sections of the dossier which will be most useful to you.

KEY	Low	You have never or not recently studied this topic, nor recently applied the concepts at work.
	Mid	You have a broad understanding of the concepts or some experience of working with them, but are not confident about your current level of knowledge.
	High	You are familiar with the concepts and their theoretical underpinning. You could confidently apply the concepts in any work context.

	Low	Mid	High
(1) Contract Management			
☞ The shared interest of client and contractor	❏	❏	❏
☞ The advantages and disadvantages of competitive tendering	❏	❏	❏
☞ Considerations organizations should bear in mind when bidding for contracts	❏	❏	❏
☞ Various types of contractual arrangement and the contexts in which they are most suitable	❏	❏	❏
☞ Standard contents and clauses of project contracts	❏	❏	❏
☞ How purchasing is managed on projects	❏	❏	❏
(2) Planning and Scheduling			
☞ The purpose and construction of the Work Breakdown Structure (WBS) and Product Breakdown Structure (PBS)	❏	❏	❏
☞ Techniques for costing project work	❏	❏	❏
☞ How Gantt and bar charts are used in project planning and scheduling	❏	❏	❏
☞ The purpose, practice and conventions of network analysis	❏	❏	❏
☞ How to plot a critical path by both the Activity on Arrow and Activity on Node method	❏	❏	❏
☞ The definition and significance of the following terms in Critical Path Analysis (CPA): precedence, dependency, dummy activities, split parallel activities, float, slack	❏	❏	❏
☞ How the critical path method may be used to find ways of reducing project time	❏	❏	❏
☞ How to analyse and present project resource requirements.	❏	❏	❏

	Low	Mid	High
(3) Implementation and Control			
☛ How project plans are translated into strategic and operational information	❏	❏	❏
☛ Various methods for communicating and reporting on project progress	❏	❏	❏
☛ How project management software can enhance project control	❏	❏	❏
☛ How to specify and introduce the right project management software	❏	❏	❏
☛ The impact of Information and Communications Technology (ICT) on project management	❏	❏	❏
☛ How ICT can be harnessed to benefit projects	❏	❏	❏
☛ Various project monitoring techniques and how these should be connected to reviews of project performance and plans	❏	❏	❏
☛ How costs are controlled on projects (including the technique of Earned Value Analysis)	❏	❏	❏
☛ Some arguments for and against exception reporting	❏	❏	❏
☛ The significance of change management procedures on projects	❏	❏	❏
☛ Techniques for identifying and addressing project problems and opportunities.	❏	❏	❏
(4) Evaluation			
☛ How to perform the principle financial evaluation methods (including Payback Time, Return on Investment, Net Present Value, Discounted Cashflow)	❏	❏	❏
☛ The purpose and construction of the Spend curve, Cumulative Cashflow diagram, Net Present Value table and Discounted Cashflow table	❏	❏	❏
☛ The purpose and application of non-financial evaluation methods including impact assessment.	❏	❏	❏

www.universal-manager.co.uk

03-1 CONTRACT MANAGEMENT

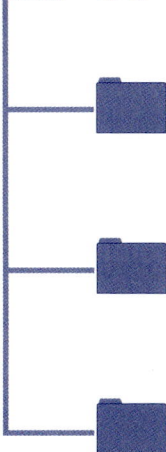

03-1 CONTRACT MANAGEMENT

'Good project contracts stay in the drawer — as soon as either party loses the confidence of the other, both parties are in trouble.'
(Curtis, Ward and Chapman, 1991)

Inherent in the nature of projects and programmes is the potential for multiple, conflicting interests. In Dossier 02, *Delivering Successful Projects*, we look at the different perspectives a typical project will encompass (including that of client, project manager and stakeholder), and at various political tactics that are often employed to further the cause of a particular party.

In project management, all too often the contract is also used as a political device:

- To shift the risk contained in the project
- To present an outward appearance of accord and progress
- To force contractors to complete poorly specified work
- To force clients to make additional payments for unspecified work.

No apologies for this pessimistic opening take on project contracts — the history of project management is littered with ill-judged attempts to use the contracting process as a blunt instrument. One inglorious example cited by Morris (1997) was the American Total Package Procurement (TPP) concept, introduced in 1966 as a way of preventing the practice among some large contractors (still prevalent today in some sectors) of 'buying-in' to contracts — in project management parlance, 'buying-in' means under-pricing contracts with the intention of securing sole supplier status for later work in the same line.

Under TPP, bids for US defence contracts were invited for a total package including systems development, production, installation and supply — contracts were awarded on a fixed price basis. The theory was that this practice would improve efficiency by increasing competition and rewarding efficiency in design, production and management. In fact what happened was that nearly all TPP contracts met with technical disaster and cost overrun (borne initially by contractors) — the rigidity of the contracts, and their failure to allow for technical and environmental risks, meant that contractors were unable to respond to the changing circumstances which affect all long term projects. The overall outcome was massive over-expenditure by the US Department of Defence which, in the cold war climate of the late 1960s and early 1970s, was compelled to bail out its struggling contractors. Total Package Procurement was abandoned in 1972.

www.universal-manager.co.uk

An effective project contract should be viewed by both involved parties as an integral part of the project's front end definition. Its agreement should coincide with the milestone of agreeing a project specification (in many projects they are one and the same, and the specification is contained in the contract). Viewed positively the contract stands for agreement between two parties on:

☞ What is to be done
☞ The scope of the contractor in carrying out that work
☞ How it will be done
☞ When it will be done
☞ How much the work is worth
☞ When and how payment will be made.

In reality though, even where it is entered into with goodwill on both sides, the contract is an adversarial device which signifies mistrust: the client doesn't trust the contractor to do the work on time, on budget and to the standards required; the contractor doesn't trust the client to pay adequately and on time! Both look to the contract for security.

Without wishing to overstate the potential for conflict they contain, it is important to identify this adversarial aspect of many contracts, and to make the point that maximizing this potential for conflict is not in the interest of the client or the contractor — but it might be in the interest of their lawyers! This is a serious point: legislative process and tradition place serious barriers in the way of clients and contractors wishing to establish productive and harmonious relationships.

PAUSE TO REFLECT

What specific legal barriers have you encountered in the context of contract management?

Now read on.

A project may be hindered in a number of ways:

☞ Failure to agree terms can of course delay work or prevent it from taking place at all

☞ Legal obfuscation in contract documents will often result in contractors and clients being at odds in their interpretation of, say, who owns the end product, what happens in the event of a delay, under what circumstances the project can be terminated by either side, and so on

☞ It is not unheard of for two contracting parties both to issue separate terms and conditions which cancel each other out

☞ Unforeseen legislative changes can add critical costs to the project — safety legislation is particularly important here.

None of these barriers is insurmountable, and the canny project manager will be wary of them and devise strategies for addressing them as early in the project life cycle as possible — for instance, gathering intelligence on impending legislation should be part of the risk analysis process for any large project. But in most cases, the project manager's first priority will be to obtain the maximum possible benefit from the project (including the contracting process) — occasionally this may involve balancing the desire to establish good working relations with the client, with the need to achieve an outcome which will deliver some strategic benefit to the contractor.

03-1-1   Tendering and Bidding

Competitive tendering became widespread in the UK during the 1980s, and it is now very unusual to acquire a contract with a publicly funded body, which is worth more than £10,000, and which does not go through some form of tendering process. Private organizations are less constrained in this respect, but many will apply a similar approach of going out to tender for projects over a certain value.

On the surface, competitive tendering offers many advantages to the client:

☞ *Selection*. In theory the tendering organization will be able to select the best contractor for the job
☞ *Cost efficiency*. Competition encourages bidders to arrive at a price attractive to the client
☞ *Innovation*. Similarly, in particularly competitive fields, bidding organizations are stimulated to adopt creative approaches.   Covertly, some organizations are not averse to using the ideas of unsuccessful bidders and treat the tendering process as a knowledge gathering exercise — this legally dubious practice is rarely punished because of the expense and difficulty of proving ownership of ideas
☞ *Specification*. For the client without a total command of key issues affecting a project, the tendering process can help to define or refine the project specification and performance measures.

PAUSE TO REFLECT

What advantages and disadvantages might there be for a bidding organization in taking part in a tendering process?

Now read on.

Planning and Controlling Projects

Ask most managers who deal with bidding for contracts about the intrinsic value of the process, and they will almost certainly emphasize the negatives:

- ☛ Time invested for no guaranteed return
- ☛ The difficulty of gauging a 'market price' for the contract under offer
- ☛ The vulnerability of ideas and tools required in bid information
- ☛ The frustration of responding within unrealistic timeframes to tender documents which contain incomplete or unclear information.

The downside of bidding for contracts should not be under-estimated, particularly for small and medium-sized businesses whose resources can scarcely be spared for what is a speculative exercise.

Of course the real prize (in normal circumstances) is in obtaining the contract, but the tendering itself may contain some benefits for bidding organizations:

- ☛ Even unsuccessful bids may raise your profile with the client organization
- ☛ It is the practice now in some government agencies to be open to all bidders about — among other things — who the tender has gone out to: so the process may be a source of market intelligence
- ☛ The knowledge generated by analysing, costing and scoping the work to be done for a contract may be useful in future: perhaps in responding to similar tenders, or possibly in the organization's own product or service development.

Tendering and bidding are complex processes which will be discussed further in Section 03-1-2 on contracts. For the rest of this section, we will examine non-contractual aspects of preparing bids.

ACTION **ACTIVITY 1**

03-1

What process is in place in your organization for assessing and preparing bids? In particular, what considerations will affect:

☞   Whether a bid is submitted at all
☞   Who is involved in preparing the bid
☞   The price quoted?

Now read on.

Bidding for Contracts

For any organization involved in the submission of proposals for contracts, the ideal process would require no more than a quote for a standard product or service. Of course, in project management this is never the case. The decision making processes entailed (in both appraising the tender and preparing the submission) need to account for a range of factors including:

(a) *The organization's strategic plan*

Will the contract on offer help achieve strategic objectives? Will it help to develop the organization (perhaps in terms of its knowledge or skills)? Will it help to open up new markets or consolidate its position within existing markets?

(b) *The macro and micro climates*

What macro factors will have a bearing on the contract? For instance a medium or long range IT or ICT-based project will need to take account of likely developments in the processing speed of computers, and of projections for greater connection speed and wider Internet accessibility year on year; a contract to build a nuclear power plant cannot start until the full environmental impact of the site, its emissions and waste disposal policy have been fully considered. Micro climate factors are to do with the state of affairs within the company: how successfully it is trading, its prospects, how well key staff are settled, and so on.

(c) *The client*

Some pertinent questions to ask will include: what do we know about the client and what can we find out; are they reputable and financially secure; do they have experience of managing similar projects; if so, have they been successful? Some clients may be a little fazed by the role reversal implicit in being asked such questions directly — but a client who has organized the tendering process effectively will have no problem responding openly.

So tell me Mr Bradshaw, what would you see as the main characteristics of an effective Chief Executive?

(d)   Competition

Forward thinking companies now dedicate some resource to Competitive Intelligence (CI). This is the — legal — practice of finding out what competitors are up to and can employ a variety of methods from 'watching' competitors' web sites (it is amazing how much commercially sensitive information is posted) to retaining research firms to provide regular reports on competitors' plans and movements.

(e)   Staffing

This factor is especially relevant in declining industry sectors, where one of the prime motives for responding to tenders is to avoid laying off sections of the workforce. This motive is partly but not entirely philanthropic: the costs of redeployment, redundancy packages and of re-hiring when the work is available are considerable. So the aim is to achieve a steady flow of work in order to achieve a stable workforce.

03-1-2   Contracts

First, the basics: in project management, a contract may take various forms. It could be expressed in a standard or a customized legal document; a purchase order or simply in an exchange of letters. In pure legal terms, a contract can be offered and entered into verbally, but this is extremely unlikely to occur for a project or programme.

The agreement set out in the contract must contain four components to be legally binding. These are the subject of our next activity.

ACTIVITY 2

The four required components are listed below. With reference to any contracts you have managed or are currently managing, what do you understand by these terms?

(a)   Intention

(b)   Offer and acceptance

(c)   Consideration

(d)   Capacity

Compare your response with our commentary in Appendix 1.

There is a variety of different types of contract in current use — each with its own merits and disadvantages. Perhaps the most important source of variation is in payment structure. Below we have listed some of the main forms of contractual payment arrangement:

Fixed price. The contractor quotes a full price for the work under offer. There may be scope for re-negotiation or later variation, but in general the contractor is required to account for all costs in the quotation.

Reimbursable. The client pays the contractor for all costs and expenses incurred in delivering the project. There are sub-variations on this type of payment structure.

Simple. Under this arrangement the contractor charges only for costs and expenses and makes no profit.

Cost-plus. With this more common form of reimbursable contract, the charging rates agreed to meet contractor costs and expenses are marked up (by agreement) to afford the contractor a margin of profit.

Schedule of rates. These are like cost-plus contracts but with the charging rate fixed to units of work performed and paid out by the client according to pre-determined schedule.

Reimbursable plus management fee. As the name implies, this is an arrangement where the contractor's profit comes from a fixed fee rather than a charging rate linked to costs. Therefore the contractor's profit does not rise with the volume of costs.

Target price. Similar to fixed price contracts, this format allows for adjustment of the price if costs are significantly greater or smaller than the original fixed fee. Of course, this adjustment cannot be made until the project is well advanced, and it is usual to make it at the end of a project when final project costs are established.

ACTION **ACTIVITY 3**

Which of the contract types described have you met? Does your organization use payment structures we have not mentioned?   Identify the payment structures of which you have experience and consider:

(a)   Their advantages

(b)   Their disadvantages

(c)   The contexts in which they work best

Now read on.

The two most common types of contract in project management today are the Fixed Price (FP) and Cost Plus Fixed Fee (CPFF). In our analysis of contract types we will concentrate on these two variations.

Fixed Price (FP)

The main advantages of this type of contract from the client's perspective are that:

☛   Price comparison between competing bids is simple
☛   Even if the client is not fully aware of the market price for the work on offer, an effective tendering process will tend to produce a cluster of bids comparable in price
☛   The risk for managing the budget falls entirely to the contractor.

For the contractor, there are two conflicting imperatives:

☞ Before the project. To come up with the most attractive bid (which tends to mean the lowest or least suspiciously low)

☞ During the project. To minimize costs so that a healthy profit margin is protected.

The tension between these two motives can, all too often, result in a project which fails, either because the contractor cannot live up to the low price quoted, or because quality is sacrificed during implementation.

The opportunity offered by profits which are linked to minimizing costs represents an 'upside' risk to the contractor. The flipside is that, if costs are too heavy, the contractor is exposed to failure and even bankruptcy.

Therefore, although a fixed price may appear attractive in its simplicity and absence of risk to the client, the actual cost if the process is not very carefully managed may be several times the original quotation, when you account for:

☞ The cost of salvaging a sunken project
☞ Claims from the contractor for unspecified costs.

Fixed price contracts are ill-advised where the work on offer contains a high degree of uncertainty. But where there is a visible history, and where the contractor has a good track record and reputation, fixed price contracts can work well.

Cost Plus Fixed Fee (CPFF)

With this arrangement the client pays a fixed fee plus all identified costs which may include:

☞ Materials, labour and equipment
☞ But also, the cost of errors, omissions, and unforeseen hitches.

For the client CPFF does have the merit that costs are directly linked to need and (if carefully monitored) the contractor should not be able to make excessive profits. But the project risk is entirely on the client side with this form of contract.

CPFF does not provide any great incentive to the contractor to work to deadlines or to the agreed quality specification. There is plenty of room for 'padding' of payment claims: with unnecessary purchases, over-staffing and dubious supply arrangements. And of course there is a deal of security in knowing that costs are covered (in fact, the issue of exactly which costs are reimbursable is likely to be the subject of negotiation — the contractor will tend to move for items like management time and overheads to be considered within the fixed fee, since these are often hard to isolate within claims for payment).

A tight specification, itemizing acceptable costs and clear on what makes up the fixed fee, is crucial to make this form of contracting work. It tends to be used where costs are not wholly predictable and where timescales are not particularly tight. Research and development projects often adopt them, as do some engineering and construction projects. But with the trend in most markets for faster 'churn' of products and services, CPFF is unlikely to attain greater popularity.

Hybrid Contracts

It might reasonably be concluded from the two preceding descriptions, that the two most common forms of contract are not especially effective. In fact there is a form of contract which is in effect a hybrid of the two, devised to get the best of both.

PAUSE TO REFLECT

Where do think the cross-over from fixed price to cost plus payment structure should occur?

Now read on.

The usual form of hybrid contract uses Cost Plus to the point where a realistic product or service has been specified, and where a full analysis of project risks has been completed and agreed by the client and contractor. Thereafter, with as much uncertainty as possible removed from the project, the Fixed Price contract will kick in.

Sharing the Risk

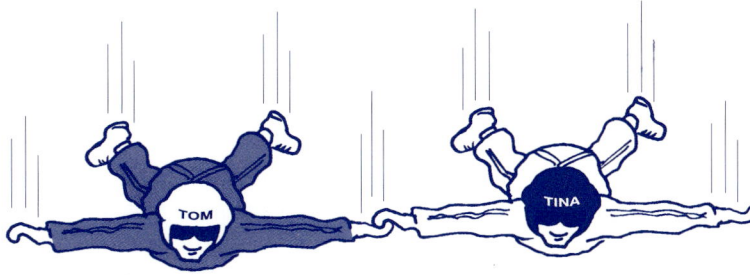

It should be clear from our discussion of contracts so far, that a critical factor in the relationship between client and contractor is where the project risk is allocated. Negotiations over contract tend to involve (usually implicit) attempts to shift risk between the two parties. Mature payment structures recognize this and aim at sharing the risk equitably.

We have already come across one example of risk sharing in this section: the Target Price form of contract which allows for contract value to be adjusted after final project costs have been audited. This means that the client can proceed without fear of paying too much for the contractor's work, while the contractor is reassured that excess costs will be met. Even this form of contract is not infallible, particularly where acceptable costs are not clearly defined, or where the contractor's cashflow is unstable.

Another instance of risk sharing is seen in the 'partnering' arrangements pioneered, according to Morris (1997), in the Japanese automotive industry during the early 1980s. The practice of partnering has spread to Europe and the UK and has been widely adopted in the retail industry, although many remain unconvinced about its practicality (particularly those suppliers who have seen their arrangements reneged upon).

Partnering involves the establishment of long term relationships, cemented by long term contracts. Taking the long view over the supply and demand relationship between client and contractor in this way can deliver some attractive benefits:

- The client will obtain quantifiable improvements over time in the value of goods or services supplied
- The client also has first (perhaps exclusive) call on the contractor's services
- Uncertainty is viewed as a joint problem and addressed jointly — neither side has to worry about over-charging or non-payment
- The relationship can develop a mutual familiarity notable in shared goals, vocabulary, practices and systems. Costs of adjusting for incompatible systems are therefore removed

☛ For the contractor, the biggest incentive of a partnering arrangement is in the security of guaranteed employment and income, and there are also likely to be benefits associated with the supplier's prestige, and likely enhancement in the skills and knowledge of staff.

The Small Print

Although legal training is not a normal requirement for project managers, they do need to pay some attention to the actual construction and wording of contracts, particularly if they work for a smaller organization without the luxury of a legal department.

A standard contract will contain most, if not all, of the following elements:

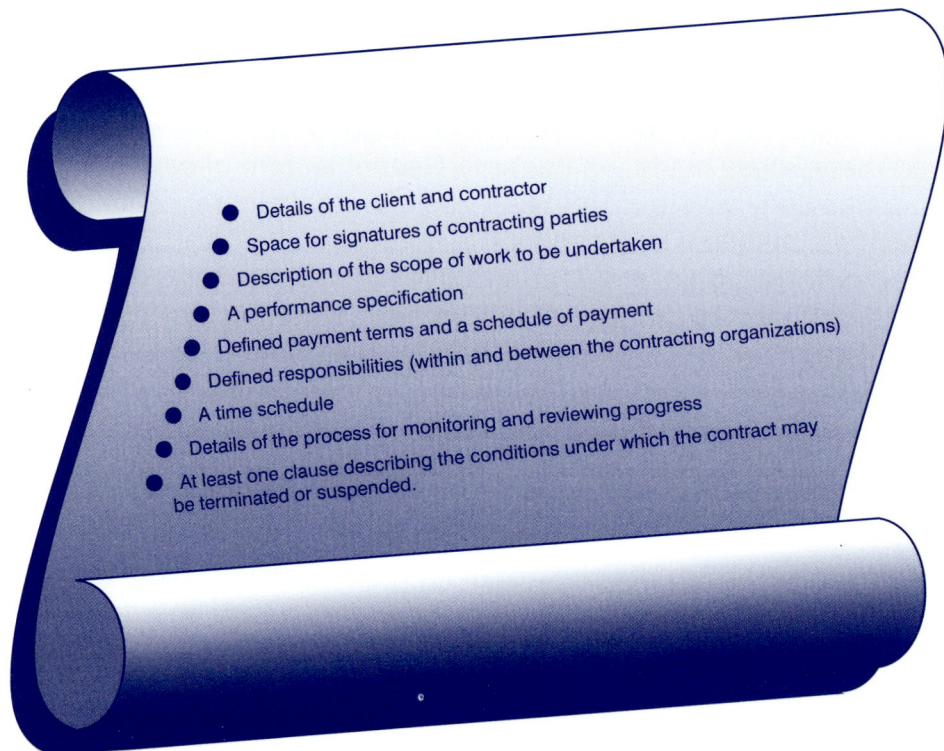

- Details of the client and contractor
- Space for signatures of contracting parties
- Description of the scope of work to be undertaken
- A performance specification
- Defined payment terms and a schedule of payment
- Defined responsibilities (within and between the contracting organizations)
- A time schedule
- Details of the process for monitoring and reviewing progress
- At least one clause describing the conditions under which the contract may be terminated or suspended.

In addition there will be a selection of the following clauses as appropriate to the type of contract:

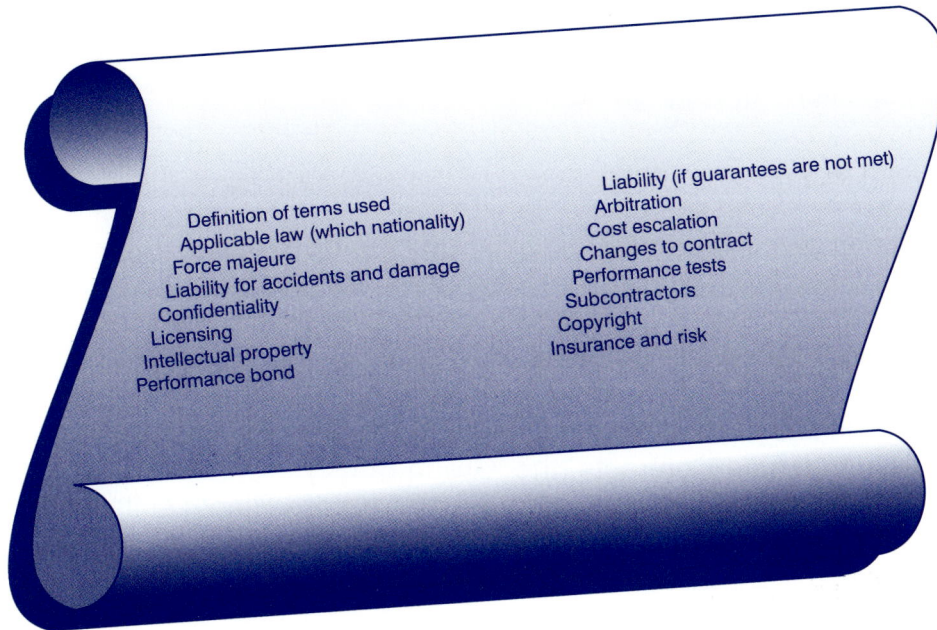

Definition of terms used
Applicable law (which nationality)
Force majeure
Liability for accidents and damage
Confidentiality
Licensing
Intellectual property
Performance bond

Liability (if guarantees are not met)
Arbitration
Cost escalation
Changes to contract
Performance tests
Subcontractors
Copyright
Insurance and risk

ACTION **ACTIVITY 4**

Re-read the list of clauses above. Are there any you are unfamiliar with?

There are descriptions of all the clauses in our commentary in Appendix 1.

There are various industry specific contracts available for unaltered use or customization. Examples from the world of engineering and construction include:

Association of Consulting Engineers (ACE)

☞ Conditions of Engagement

Institution of Civil Engineers

☞ Conditions of Contract for Civil Engineering Works
☞ Conditions of Contract for Design and Construction

Institution of Chemical Engineers

☞ Conditions of Contract for Complete Process Plants suitable for Reimbursable Contracts (the 'Green Book')
☞ Conditions of Contract for Complete Process Plants suitable for Lump Sum Contracts (the 'Red Book')

ACTION **ACTIVITY 5**

Find out if there are any standard contracts pertinent to your industry sector. A good place to start your enquiry would be the Internet where associations and lead bodies affiliated to your sector are likely to have web sites.

Now read on.

03-1-3 Purchasing

We close this opening section with a brief look at the practice of purchasing as it applies to project management.

Many project costs are in-house (e.g. salaries, wages and overheads). However, a considerable proportion of expenditure on large or medium-sized projects will be for purchasing labour (professional, skilled and unskilled), materials and equipment. Discrete work packages will almost certainly be subcontracted, and labour may be purchased directly from self-employed people or through an agency.

Price is not the only factor in efficient purchasing. To avoid quality problems and delays it is crucial that the project manager is assured of the reliability, expertise, capacity and financial stability of all suppliers. One way to ensure the kind of service required is to develop partnering arrangements of the type described in section 03-1-2 — long term relationships with suppliers should in theory lead to efficient, up to standard delivery. On the other hand, it may also lead to complacency on both sides: frequent turn-over or at least frequent re-appraisal of supply relationships has the merit of keeping prices, and possibly methods, keen.

The starting point of the purchasing or procurement process is the purchase order. This will contain information such as serial numbers to identify the goods; the agreed purchase price quoted by the supplier and accepted by the purchaser; delivery details such as place, conditions and most importantly date; invoicing instructions and an authorizing signature.

PURCHASE ORDER   No. 446/

Name & Address of Buyer   Date: /   /

To   _____

Address   _____

            _____

            _____

Item No.	Description	Quantity	Price

Method of delivery

Delivery date: /   /   Signature . . . .

Terms and Conditions are supplied overleaf.

The offer of goods or material and acceptance of the offer is a binding legal contract and the conditions of contract need to be understood by both parties. After an order has been placed, regular follow-up is advisable to ensure that there are no delays or to provide early warning to the project manager if any delay is likely. There may also be a requirement for inspection to ensure that the required quality criteria are being met.

Packing, transport and insurance are important risk areas and areas of significant cost. For instance, large construction projects will probably require specialist transport; for large and heavy loads, police permission is required to transport by road, and cranes may need to be hired to handle goods or materials after delivery. Goods need to be insured during transit and a key question (which should be addressed in the contract) is who is responsible for the cost of insurance and freight:

- ☛ If the price of goods is a 'factory gate price', the purchaser will be responsible for collecting, transporting and insuring
- ☛ The contract may be for delivery to the client site, in which case the vendor is responsible.

For smaller delivery carriers, couriers and postal services may be used and the same attention to responsibility for the cost of insurance and delivery needs to be clear.

Procurement

In large firms, the procurement department (or buying department) is responsible for the actions described above (in smaller firms project managers may have to handle procurement themselves with administrative back-up). The procurement manager's job is more than simply buying. He or she will handle a purchase like a project. The procurement department will keep records of past purchases and from these develop lists of approved suppliers with a proven track record of reliability, quality and value for money. After order placement, the procurement manager still has a responsibility that doesn't end until delivery of the equipment, material or service.

In many large and medium-sized organizations, the purchase requisition is the document that starts the purchasing process. It originates when the appropriate individual or department provides a specification for what is required (in construction and engineering projects this may involve provision of detailed drawings). The requisition is in effect a request for the procurement department to obtain quotations from preferred suppliers along with the conditions for transport, insurance, delivery, and a specification of payment terms. The request will also ask for the suppliers' quality standards, or an agreement to work to defined standards. From a project management point of view delivery, cost and assurance on quality will be the key elements sought. Where equipment, material or services are specialized there may be only one possible supplier but normally the procurement manager will obtain alternative quotations.

On the basis of the bids obtained a technical and commercial bid analysis will be carried out by the technical specialist and cost accounts. Positive and negative features will be given scores, ideally in money terms, to determine the best value. The legal terms of the purchase will be examined by the procurement department and in the case of involved conditions of contract by the legal department.

Life Cycle Costing

Life cycle costing is now being regularly imposed on suppliers. This is an evaluation process that has sustainability at its core. It looks not only at the initial cost but also at the cost over the life of the product to be supplied, right through to its final disposal:

- ☛ How much energy will it use in its lifetime
- ☛ How much maintenance and what spare parts will it need
- ☛ What will it cost to dispose of
- ☛ Will its component parts be capable of being recycled?

As well as issues like these, the project manager will get more and more involved in future in the related issues of more rigorous safety and environmental controls on items to be purchased.

Purchase Orders

Once the best supplier has been identified using the bid analysis criteria described above, a purchase order is raised. On receiving this, the supplier should acknowledge it, confirming the terms of purchase. This acknowledgement will be compared with the original bid terms and any negotiated changes. Any discrepancies will be queried. A legally binding contract now exists. The next action on the part of the buyer is to *expedite* or follow up the purchase in the period between order and delivery. This is to ensure that work is continuing at the supplier's place of work and that the programme is being adhered to. The person responsible for expediting the purchase will note any likely delays and relay these to the project manager. The same person should also liaise with whoever is responsible for goods inspection to ensure the equipment or goods meet quality and safety standards.

ACTION **ACTIVITY 6**

The purchasing processes and issues described above are of most relevance to large and medium-sized organizations. How much of our description varies with practice where you work?

Now read on.

03-2 PLANNING AND SCHEDULING

03-2

03-2 PLANNING AND SCHEDULING

Project planning is the evaluation of the time and effort to complete a project. It takes into account all resources available - human resources, money, materials, machines and equipment, etc. It may therefore be more accurate to define project planning as the prediction of the time to complete a project, taking into account all resource constraints.

The planning process considers all the individual tasks that make up the project, the time each takes, the interdependence and precedence of project tasks and the resources each task will draw upon. Since resources are usually limited, the planner's art is often about finding the most efficient use of resources from a number of alternatives.

For other than the simplest projects, the plan must be committed to paper or stored as a computer file. It must be drawn up to established rules if it is to be used by more than one person. The more thought that goes into the plan at the earliest stages, when least is known about the project, the less chance there will be of disaster later.

03-2-1 What Has to be Done

A project consists of a number of related activities, some of which cannot be started until others are completed and some that can run in parallel. The most common starting point in the planning process is therefore to establish all the activities that will constitute the project. It is advisable to do this uncritically at first, without questioning the relationships between activities too deeply — in time the initial chaos should settle into a logical breakdown of activities and their linkages.

At this early stage it is useful to involve key people who will have responsibility for executing the major parts of the project and to brainstorm what has to be done (WHTBD). Checklists from previous, similar projects may be helpful, but many successful project teams will go into the WHTBD session(s) armed with nothing more than a fistful of biros and post-it notes — these are sufficient for the essential job which is to define the tasks and begin to establish their relationships.

There are two related tools widely used to impose some order on this potentially chaotic process.

Work Breakdown Structure (WBS)

The WBS is a tool for deconstructing the project down to a level where discrete tasks have been identified whose execution can be planned and controlled. It tends to take a 'parent-child' structure (with all the potential extensions inherent within that structure). Below a simple WBS is illustrated, taking as an example, an outline process for publishing a book.

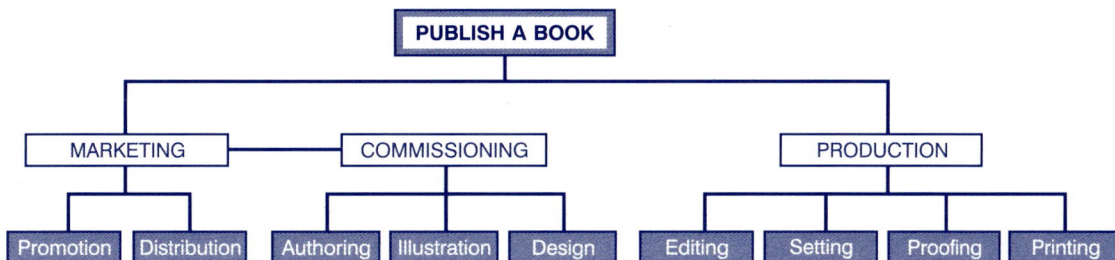

```
                        ┌─────────────────┐
                        │ PUBLISH A BOOK  │
                        └────────┬────────┘
          ┌──────────────────────┼──────────────────────────┐
   ┌──────────────┐      ┌──────────────┐            ┌──────────────┐
   │  MARKETING   │──────│ COMMISSIONING│            │  PRODUCTION  │
   └──────┬───────┘      └──────┬───────┘            └──────┬───────┘
     ┌────┴────┐        ┌───────┼────────┐      ┌──────┬────┴──┬───────┐
 Promotion Distribution Authoring Illustration Design Editing Setting Proofing Printing
```

Key points to note from this example are:

☞ The top level is reserved for the project's overall purpose

☞ The next level describes major parts of the project (already at this level it is common that critical relationships are identified — in our example, commissioning cannot begin until marketing has established the need for a book)

☞ At the lowest level, work packages are identified which are capable of being carried out by individual people, teams or sub-contractors (it is most helpful for planning and control if the WBS is taken down to this level, where discrete contributions can be plotted and measured)

☞ In our example, we have not begun the refining activity of establishing links between the work packages — this is not really the job of the WBS. However, the process of defining the breakdown of activities is a helpful prompt for analysing dependency (when one activity cannot start until another is completed) and precedence (the reverse — an activity must finish before another starts). In our illustration, you can see the beginnings of this analysis with, for example, production activities placed to the right of commissioning activities, but there are more complex, iterative relationships for which the WBS is not an appropriate presentation format (e.g. the relationships between authoring and design, editing and authoring, etc.)

Product Breakdown Structure (PBS)

Similar in format to the WBS, the Product Breakdown Structure is used to identify the components of a product. At its most useful it will break down a complex or detailed construction into its smallest parts (so a bicycle for instance would be stripped down to the level of ball bearings and spokes).   If we attempt to create a PBS for the project analysed previously in our WBS, it's evident that the PBS is not required for simple, predictable artefacts like books. However, the PBS approach could usefully be applied to specific parts of the book publishing project, such as the authoring.

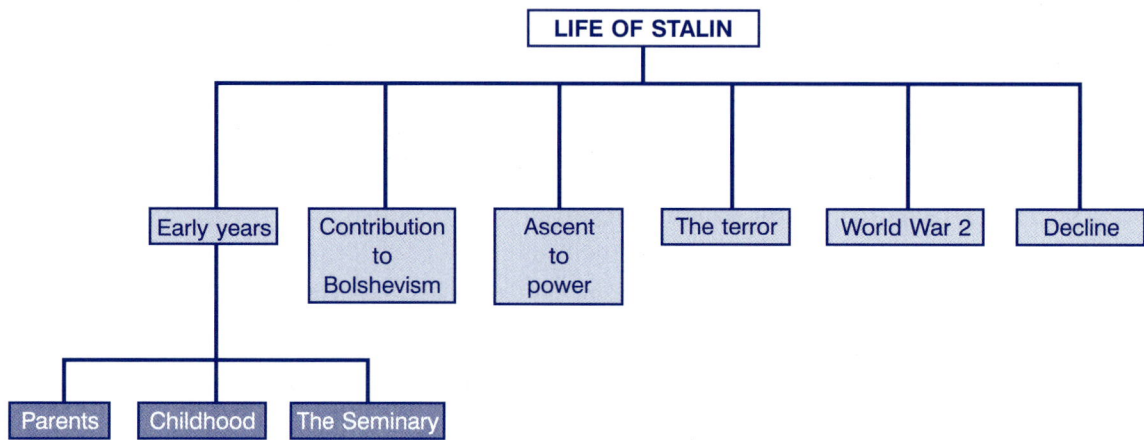

```
                          LIFE OF STALIN
   ┌──────────┬──────────┬──────────┬──────────┬──────────┐
Early years  Contribution  Ascent    The terror  World War 2  Decline
              to          to
              Bolshevism  power
   ┌──────────┼──────────┐
Parents    Childhood   The Seminary
```

The PBS is an excellent tool for planning complex products such as motor vehicles or software programs. In such instances, it may be used as the starting point for creation of the WBS, so that each identified component would be further broken down in terms of the work needed to acquire it.

Both the PBS and WBS formats can also contribute to project costing and control. At a simple level, this would involve putting an estimated resource requirement for each component or work package specified (costs for components, manpower for work packages). But once confident that the structure is definitive, the project manager may also assign codes to each component or work package, as in the example shown on the next page. These may subsequently be used in the allocation of budget codes to the project.

Project 19:   Move to new premises
        19.1 Establish budget
              19.1.1   Finalize business plan
              19.1.2   Consult bank
              19.1.3   Investigate alternative finance arrangements
              19.1.4   Fix budget

        19.2 Identify new premises
              19.2.1   Agree requirements
              19.2.2   Investigate options
              19.2.3   Decision

        19.3 Arrange new facilities
              19.3.1   Agree new requirements
              19.3.2   Set up new arrangements
              19.3.3   Transfer existing arrangements

03-2

03-2-2   Costing the Job

As a project proceeds through the 'initiate' and 'specify' stages, more than one estimate is likely to be required of its cost. The basis for any estimate will be the project's specification (provided initially by the client and gradually refined by the project manager in consultation with the client and others with an interest in the project.) The specification and estimate will therefore develop in parallel until the point where a definitive decision is made to pursue the project.

Types of Estimate

There are various models of estimate which become progressively more accurate:

- Order of Magnitude Estimate (accuracy greater than ± 30%)
- Study Estimate (accuracy up to ± 30%)
- Preliminary Estimate (accuracy ± 20%)
- Definitive Estimate (accuracy ± 10%)
- Detailed Estimate (accuracy ±5%).

Added to the above, some large projects also prepare an 'As Built Estimate' at the end of the job. This sets out the actual cost to complete the project and is the one figure that can be of high accuracy. Analysis of this figure against estimates and budgets will give valuable information, and should be retained as a guide for future estimates.

As well as providing a prediction of the cost to complete the project, the Detailed Estimate later becomes the basis for controlling the project. It is used to prepare the *Control Estimate* or Budget. During the project, a continuous comparison will be made of actual against planned expenditure as set out in the Control Estimate.

Other classifications in use, with their supposed accuracy, are Ball Park (± 25%), Comparative (± 15%), Feasibility (± 10%) and Definitive (± 5%). Some organizations develop their own definitions for estimate types.

ACTION **ACTIVITY 7**

What are the main costs incurred by projects carried out by your organization?

Compare your response with our commentary in Appendix 1.

Costing Models

Individual organizations tend to have their own costing methods, taking account of the factors listed previously and additional, specialized items. These are either based on the company's registered experience of project management, or are standard methods for the industry. A *current* formula has the advantages of ensuring that nothing vital is missed and that calculations are consistent — keeping formulae current can be challenging, though, with continuous developments in areas like taxation and energy costs. It is therefore important to interrogate costing models before applying them, to test their accuracy and coverage in relation to your project activities.

An example from the chemical plant construction industry would use many of the headings already discussed as well as:

☛ Buildings and Structures	—	Steel, Brick and Concrete
☛ Piping	—	A sub-heading of materials
☛ Instruments	—	A specific area of equipment
☛ Electrics	—	Transformers, motors, cables, etc.
☛ Shipping		
☛ Transport		
☛ Insurance.		

03-2

The last three can amount to a significant proportion of a large project — 10% would not be unusual.

ACTION ACTIVITY 8

Describe the model used for cost estimating in your own organization and highlight any methods that are specific to your area.

Now read on.

03-2-3   Timing of Projects

Project planning establishes the relationship between the time allowed to complete a project and the time needed, and enables the project manager to assess the leeway for adjustments to planned activity.

Planning and Controlling Projects

Having established the activities the project will contain (using the WBS, PBS or both), the next step is to assign estimated durations to each activity. The deadline for completion is usually fixed, but it is often possible to re-schedule by changing the sequence in which the tasks are done, while still retaining the original estimates — this is why it is so important to establish dependency and precedence between activities.

There are alternatives to this process of manipulating the sequence of activities:

☞ Acquire more resources
☞ Acquire faster, cheaper or more productive resources
☞ Negotiate over deadlines.

But, if available, these alternatives need to be explored and discussed with the client at an early stage in project planning. Achieving a project in the shortest possible time is usually the most cost effective option, and the one most attractive to the client.

There is however a parallel danger of trying, or being persuaded, to attempt to complete a job within an unrealistic timeframe. This trap looms largest in competitive situations, or where the project managing organization is in an insecure position — it very rarely results in project success.

Gantt or Bar Charts

The oldest planning method is the bar chart, also known as a Gantt chart (after Henry Gantt who developed this tool for production scheduling in 1917). That it has survived so long as a project management tool, is in part due to its simplicity: Gantt charts are easy to construct and interpret. They plot time along the top of a scale, against project activities down the left hand side.

Below is a simple example of a table often used for planning and scheduling projects — it outlines the tasks in a small building project, and gives their anticipated durations and an indication of which tasks are dependent upon the completion of others.

Task	Description	Dependency	Duration
A	Apply for Planning Approval	—	2 days
B	Hire Builders	—	1 day
C	Clear Site	A,B	5 days
D	Lay Foundations	C,E,G	7 days
E	Order Building Materials	—	1 day
F	Build Wall	D	4 days
G	Remove Soil	C	2 days

www.universal-manager.co.uk

A Gantt chart developed from this table would look like this:

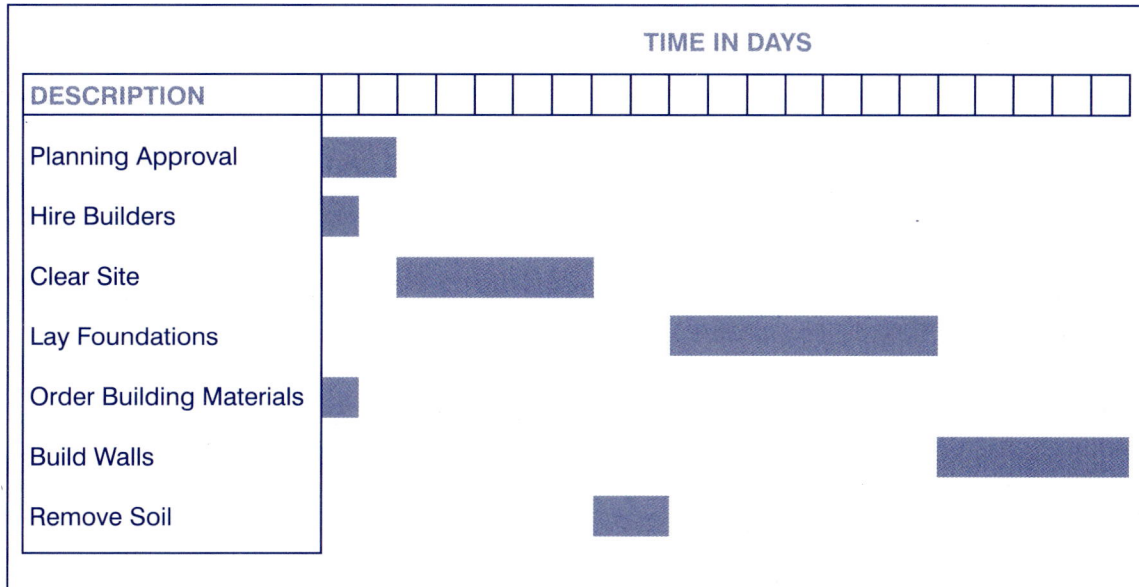

DESCRIPTION	TIME IN DAYS
Planning Approval	
Hire Builders	
Clear Site	
Lay Foundations	
Order Building Materials	
Build Walls	
Remove Soil	

The Gantt chart is widely used in project management, and is one of the main presentation formats used in project management software (we will return to the subject of software in section 03-3-3). The format is sufficiently flexible to allow individual refinements: for instance many project managers use colour or shading to denote resource identities; others use the chart to monitor progress by showing the position of each activity at the current date.

v

ACTIVITY

The bar above shows an Activity which is 30% complete. If 'v' indicates the current date, the chart also shows that the activity is behind schedule.

ACTION ACTIVITY 9

As an aid to project planning, what shortcomings do you think the Gantt or bar chart has?

Compare your response with ours in the commentary in Appendix 1.

ACTION ACTIVITY 10

Prepare a Gantt chart for a simple project which you might undertake. You need not restrict yourself to the workplace here — for instance, a small home improvement job would be ideal for this exercise.

Now read on.

03-2-4   Project Network Analysis

The bar chart has many limitations for the scheduling of complex projects. The Critical Path Method (CPM) using the Critical Path Network is a more powerful tool. The process is called Critical Path Analysis (CPA).

Network Diagrams

A network diagram consists of nodes and links (nodes are points on a diagram and links are the lines which join them). Road and rail maps are commonplace examples of network diagrams — the towns or stations are nodes, and the roads or rail lines are the links.

Networks are not drawn to scale. In the critical path diagram, the links have arrows showing the direction the logic takes.

CPM

Credit for the invention of the Critical Path Method has gone to Du Pont who devised it in the late 1950s to plan maintenance programmes for chemical plant. It is this planning technique which we will focus on in this dossier, since it is the most widely practised by project managers.

PERT

03-2

PERT stands for 'Programme Evaluation and Review Technique' and was a forerunner of CPM (although it is less widely used today). The United States Defence Department developed it in the 1950s for the Polaris Missile programme. Its chief divergence from CPM is in the way the activity time is derived: instead of requiring a single figure for task duration, the PERT system calls for three different times to be estimated (namely the expected task duration, the optimistic version and the pessimistic version). A weighted mean figure is then calculated from these three variants.

We will not elaborate further on the PERT method in this dossier, mainly because, by comparison with CPM, it is rarely used by project managers today.

03-2-5   Critical Path Networks

With the Critical Path Method, there are two methods of representation:

☛ *Activity on Arrow.* Here the nodes are events or points in time, probably weeks or months from the project's start. The links are activities which take defined periods to complete (represented as arrows). For manual drawing of Critical Path Networks, this type of representation appears to be the most widely used, and historically was the first. It is often referred to as *AoA* (Activity on Arrow).

☛ *Activity on Node.* The opposite approach. Nodes are activities and links are events. At first this does not look as logical, but in fact the logic is simpler and is more suited to computer programming. Often referred to as *AoN* (Activity on Node).

Planning and Controlling Projects

Characteristics of a CPM Network

For the remainder of this section, in the main we will employ the AoA technique.

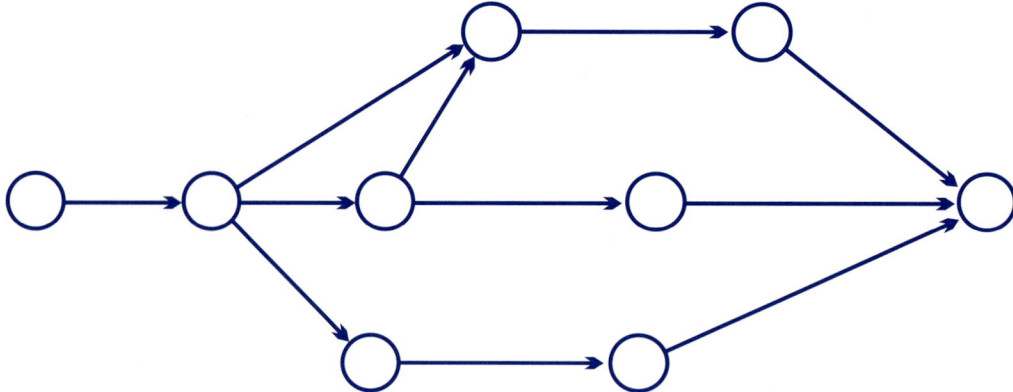

A fundamental point in a network is that there can only be one link between any two nodes. There is a trick for dealing with situations where more than one activity links two events which we will describe shortly.

Representation is by an arrow diagram and the final diagram is required to:

- Present information graphically
- Identify the order in which tasks should be carried out
- Identify the interdependence between tasks
- Estimate how long the project will take
- Identify when each activity must be finished
- Show the maximum delay (float) allowable for each activity without adverse consequences for the project
- Facilitate scheduling of resources
- Monitor and control activities
- Allow for adjustments.

Activities

Activities or tasks must be uniquely identified: the duration of each individual task must be known, as must the interdependency between tasks. The actual scope or content of an activity is a matter for fine judgement by the project manager — for instance, activities which involve no actual work and consume no resources sometimes still need to be plotted because they will take time (e.g. waiting for a delivery).

www.universal-manager.co.uk

Duration

Estimating duration is most effective if past experience can be factored in. The PERT approach of calculating a mean duration from three variants can be a useful approach if no track record has been established.

It is worth stressing that project managers shouldn't attempt to establish task durations in isolation, particularly where there are no suitable comparisons. It is common sense that other people with appropriate expertise can contribute to the process of estimating how long critical activities will take.

03-2

Dependency and Precedence

Often the relationships between project activities are obvious, but it is rare to avoid having to make some judgement calls. Defining dependency and precedence should not be treated as a one-off: with large or complex projects especially, it is wise to revisit and revise activity linkages several times during the 'specify' stage. Until a definitive project specification has been produced it is unlikely that all links and priorities will be uncovered.

Events

An event is the start or finish of an activity. In a critical path, more than one activity can start or finish at one event. Significant events are termed 'milestones'.

Conventions

We will take a simple example: building a brick wall. To a house builder this could be a single task, but to a bricklayer it consists of a number of activities which we have defined as: (A) Mix mortar; (B) Lay bricks; (C) Point wall.

The starting point is an activity table showing dependency and duration. Activities are given a designation (alphabetical, numerical or mixed classifications are all acceptable):

Activity	Description	Duration	Dependency
A	Mix Mortar	1	—
B	Lay Bricks	3	A
C	Point Wall	2	B

The network diagram derived from our tabulated data would be as follows:

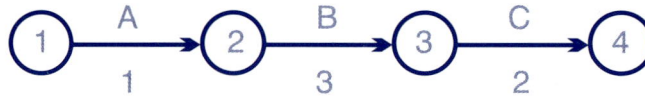

The numbers in the nodes are event numbers, i.e. points in time.

The key conventions which underpin CPM are that:

- Time flows from left to right
- Events further along the path take a higher number than earlier events
- Nodes at the start of tasks are 'head nodes'; those at the end are 'tail nodes'
- Tasks can be referred to by events on either side, i.e. B can be task 2-3
- It is not necessary for numbers to be in sequence: leaving spaces can be useful, particularly where it is known that plans are likely to be refined
- Connecting lines need not be straight, but drawn to suit layout.
- Time is normally printed under the arrows.

Dependency Rules

If two or more tasks depend on completion of a previous activity, these must all emerge from the head node of that task. An event is not realized until all tasks leading to it are completed even though some tasks may be capable of finishing before the event is realized.

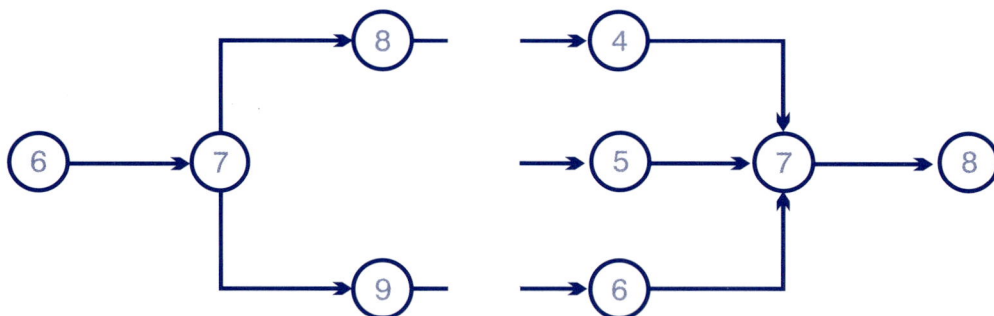

Dummies in Networks

In CPM diagrams there must be only one link (or activity) shown between two nodes (or events). This applies even if, in practice, there is more than one activity that can be carried out in parallel and between the two events. Having 'dummy' activities solves the problem.

The dummy activity is there to maintain the logic, especially in complex diagrams. It is represented by a dotted line and it is an activity of zero duration. It necessitates the addition of an extra numbered event.

Identity Dummy Activities

Consider the following extract from an activity table:

Activity	Duration	Dependency
E	2	D
F	4	D
G	5	D

Not according to rules   **Correct**

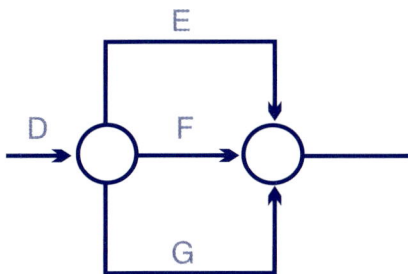

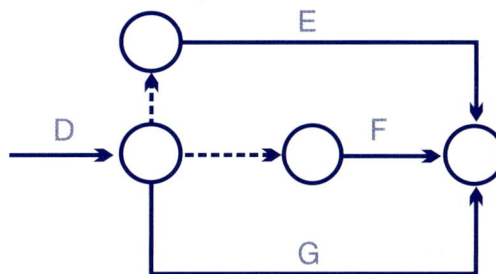

'Identity or Uniqueness Dummy' is the term for a dummy activity to deal with parallel activities between two events in CPM (using Activity on Arrow). The identity dummy can precede or follow the parallel activity with which it is associated (in most cases it follows). By convention it is added to the parallel activity with the shorter duration.

Logical Dummy Activities

Consider a situation represented by the following extract from an activity table:

Activity	Dependency
A	—
B	—
K	A
L	A, B

The following would be the usual way to plot this sequence of activities.

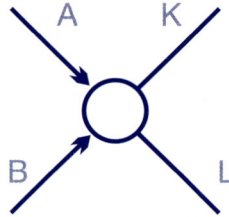

On examination, it is clear that the logic in this plotting is awry. The diagram shows that L can start only when A and B is finished, which is correct. It also shows that K can start only when A, B are finished, which is contrary to the tabulated data.

The solution is to use a 'logical dummy'.

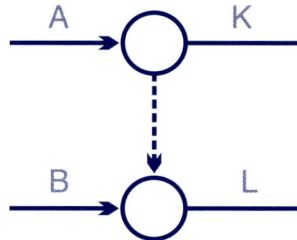

Split Parallel Activities

Often there are situations where a succeeding activity can start before the preceding one is totally completed. It is necessary to start the first activity but not necessary to finish it before the next activity begins — it can start part way through. Both activities run in parallel for part of the time. This is a special case of the logical dummy.

An example might have activity S (illustrated below) as stripping wallpaper, while activity W is washing the walls. The sequence of activities is as follows:

☞ First part of S alone
☞ Followed by S and W in parallel
☞ Followed by W on its own.

Consecutively

Part in Parallel

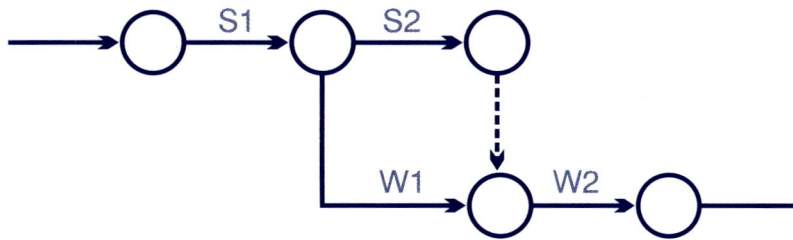

This parallel stacking of activities should be familiar to you: it is the CPM representation of concurrency.

Here is an example of a network containing both types of dummy activity, shown first in tabular form and then via CPM:

Activity	Dependency
A	—
B	A
C	A
D	B
E	C
F	C
G	D
H	E, F
I	G, H
J	I
K	H
L	K

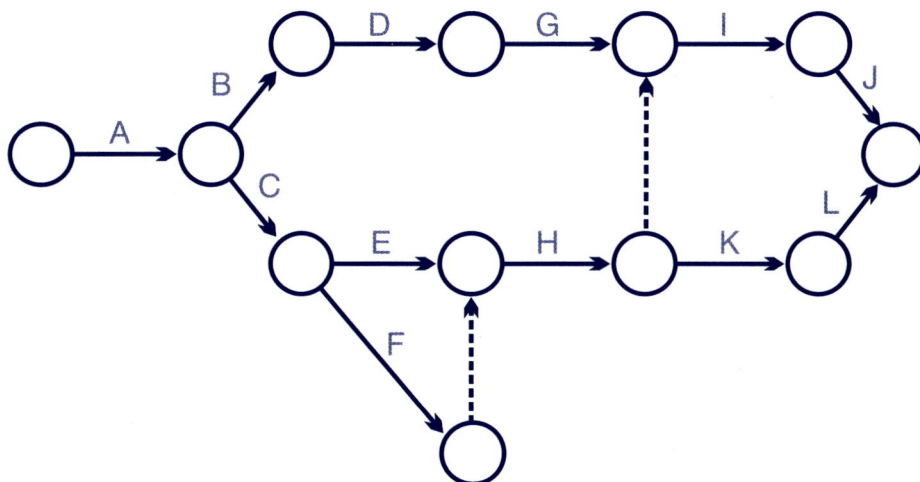

03-2-6   Critical Paths and Times

The shortest time a project can be completed in is known as 'total project time'. It is determined by the sequence of activities known as the 'critical path'. Once the timing for all possible sequences or paths from the start to the finish of the project have been plotted, the path that gives the longest time is the critical path. All other paths should contain some 'slack'.

Finding the critical path is not a particularly complex activity, but it does require concentration and familiarity with the conventions described here.

From the duration of each activity it is possible, by working through from the beginning, to arrive at the Earliest Start Time (EST) and the Earliest Finishing Time (EFT) for each activity.

$$EFT = EST + \text{activity duration}$$

The EFT for one activity is the EST for the next activity.

The Latest Start Time (LST) is the latest time an activity can start without causing a delay to the project. The Latest Finish Time (LFT) is the latest time an activity can finish and not affect the overall timing.

$$LST = LFT - \text{activity duration}$$

It is convenient to think of the timing of events in the same way, i.e. that each event can have an Earliest Event Time (EET) and a Latest Event Time (LET).

The EST of an emerging activity is the same as the EET. The LFT of an entering activity is the same as the LET.

To calculate total project time, a forward pass is made from the start to the end of the project, to give the EST using the relationship:

$$EFT = EST + \text{activity duration}$$

The Earliest Finish for one activity is the Earliest Start for the next. The process ends at the last activity and gives the Earliest Finish Times for the different routes through the project. The longest of these routes will give the total project time.

The critical path is the particular sequence of events that makes up total project time. This is found by doing a backward pass through the different sequences. The Latest Start Times for each activity are found using the relationship:

$$LST = LFT - \text{activity duration}.$$

The critical path is the one through those events where the Earliest Event Time equals the Latest Event Time. We will illustrate this process shortly, but before doing so, some conventions and terminology need to be explained. In CPM, there are a number of conventions for representing an event. Below we show two common approaches (the top one conforms to British Standard BS 4335: 1889):

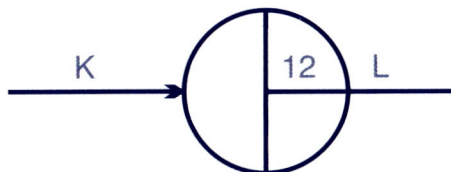

Earliest Event Time (EET)

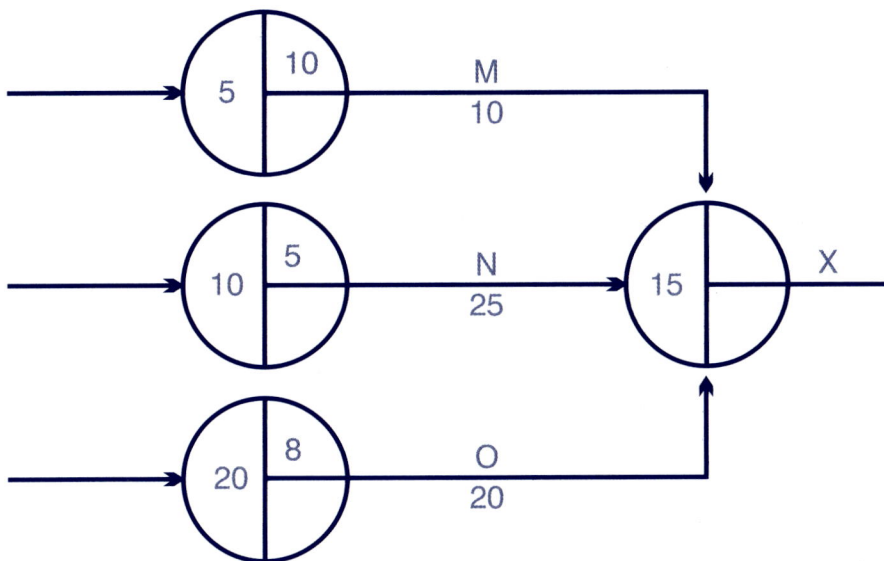

Event Number

Event Number

Latest Event Time (LET)

K   12   L   K   L
                            23

Earliest K can finish,
earliest L can start

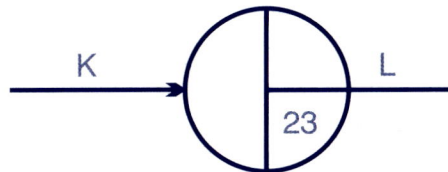

Latest K can finish,
latest L can start

Earliest Event Time

5   10   M
           10

10   5   N
          25

15   X

20   8   O
          20

In the illustration above, event 10 has an Earliest Event Time (EET) of 5 weeks, and therefore activity N has an Earliest Start Time (EST) of 5 weeks. N takes 25 weeks, therefore its Earliest Finish Time (EFT) is 5 + 25 = 30 weeks.

In the same way M has an EFT of 20 weeks and O an EFT of 28 weeks.

An event cannot be realized until all the activities leading into it are complete. Therefore the Earliest Event Time (EET) for event 15 is 30 weeks (the greatest out of 30, 20 and 28).

Latest Event Time

For this we work backwards:

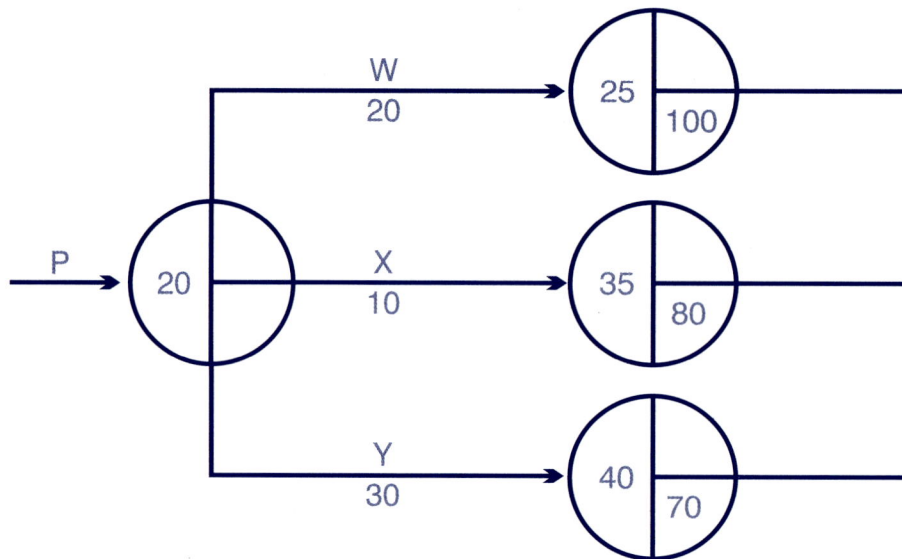

Activity Y has duration of 30 weeks. The succeeding event has a Latest Event Time (LET) of 70 weeks, or a Latest Finish Time (LFT) of 70 weeks. Therefore the Latest Start Time (LST) of activity Y is 70 – 30 = 40 weeks.

In the same way, W has an LST of 80 weeks and X an LST of 70 weeks.

Therefore the latest time that event 20 must be reached is 40 (the least out of 40, 80 and 70).

www.universal-manager.co.uk

To Obtain the Critical Path

This will be done using an example.

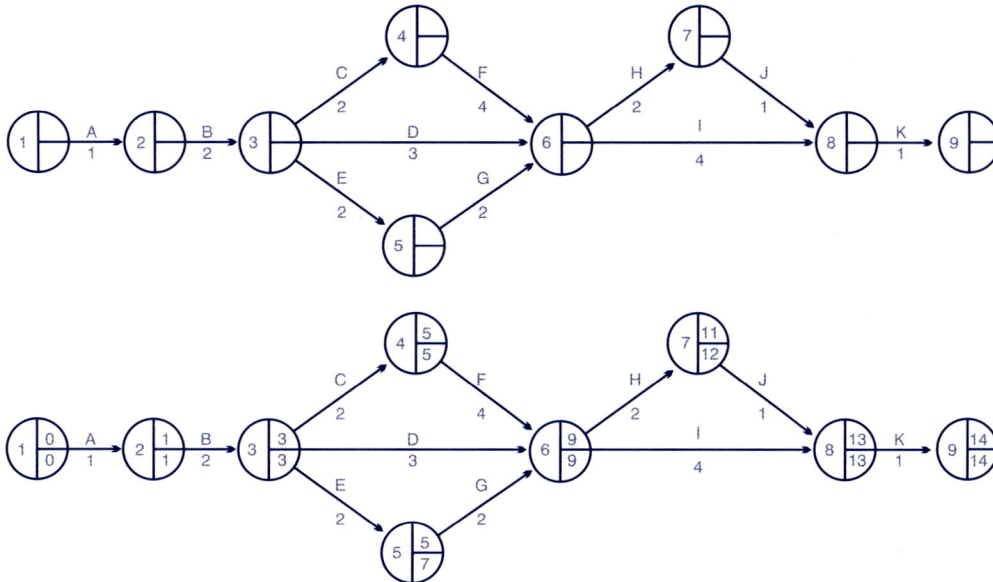

We will work forward to the end. When the Earliest Finish Time (EFT) for the last event is arrived at this is also made the Latest Finish Time (LFT), i.e. 14. Working from the last event backwards, using the method described, will give zero for the Latest Starting Time (LST) — if done correctly.

The lower of the two previous diagrams shows that the minimum time required for the project is 14 weeks.

Consider activity E. This has an Earliest Start Time (EST) of 3 weeks into the project and a Latest Finish Time (LFT) of 7 weeks. Therefore the time available is $7 - 3 = 4$ weeks. The activity has, however, a required time of 2 weeks. It therefore has a 'float' of $4 - 2 = 2$ weeks.

Similarly activity G has a float of 2 weeks, activity H has 1 week and activity J a 3 week float. Activity I on the other hand has time available of 4 weeks counterbalanced by a time required of 4 weeks: therefore it has no float. The path through those activities with no float is the critical path.

The critical path for this project is the one through A, B, C, F, I and K (i.e. the path through those events where the Earliest Event Time is equal to the Latest Event Time).

03-2-7   Activity on Arrow Networks

From the event times of the tail and head nodes we can work out for any activity:

☞   The Earliest and Latest Start Times
☞   The Earliest and Latest Finish Times.

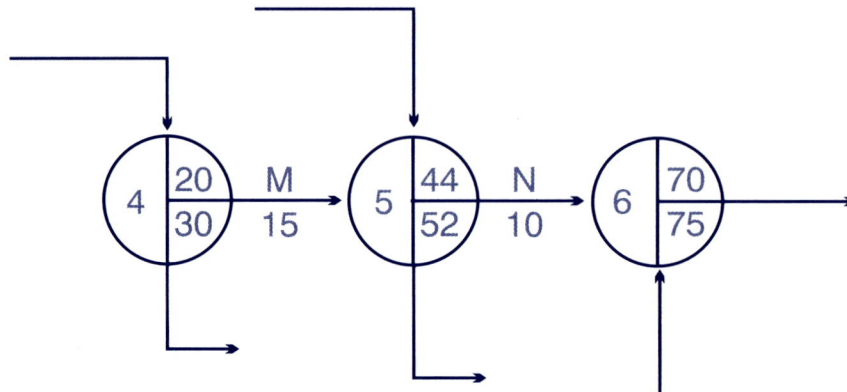

		Start Time		Finish Time	
Activity	**Duration**	**Earliest**	**Latest**	**Earliest**	**Latest**
M	15	20	37	35	52
N	10	44	65	54	75

Note: The latest start time is not the same as the latest event time. This is decided by the earliest of all the activities emerging from the tail node.

The earliest finish time is not the same as the earliest event time. This is decided by the later of all the times entering the head node.

Total Float

Consider activity M.

Latest time it can finish   = 52 weeks
Earliest time it can start   = 20
Maximum time available   = 32
Duration (time required)   = 15
Therefore the float   = 32 − 15   = 17 weeks

This is known as the 'total float'. The total float can be used either at the beginning or the end, or can be within the activity. It may be used for example to save resources (taking longer than the scheduled time by using up the float).

Similarly for activity N:

> Maximum time = 75 – 44 = 31 weeks
> Duration   = 10
> Total float   = 21 weeks

Free Float

Suppose we use up the entire float in activity M (i.e. it takes the maximum time available of 32 weeks). Then the earliest finish time is now 52 weeks. This gives for activity N:

> New maximum time   = 75 – 52 = 23 weeks
> Duration (time required)   = 10
> New float   = 13 weeks
> Whereas it had a Total Float   = 21 weeks

In other words the use of float on one activity affects the available float on another activity. The effect on activity N was caused by the new earliest time of 52 weeks. If we stick to 44 weeks the float on activity N will not be affected. How does this affect activity M?

> New maximum time for M = 44 – 20 = 24 weeks
> Duration   = 15
> New float   = 9 weeks

This is the amount of float the activity has without affecting the succeeding activity and is known as the 'free float' (in this case it is 9 weeks).

Activity M has a total float of 17 weeks and a free float of 9 weeks.

Free float is the total extent by which an activity can be delayed without affecting a succeeding activity.

By the same reasoning activity N has a total float of 21 weeks and a free float of 16 weeks.

(d) If reduction costs £1,000 per week what would the cost of reducing the project to 18 weeks be?

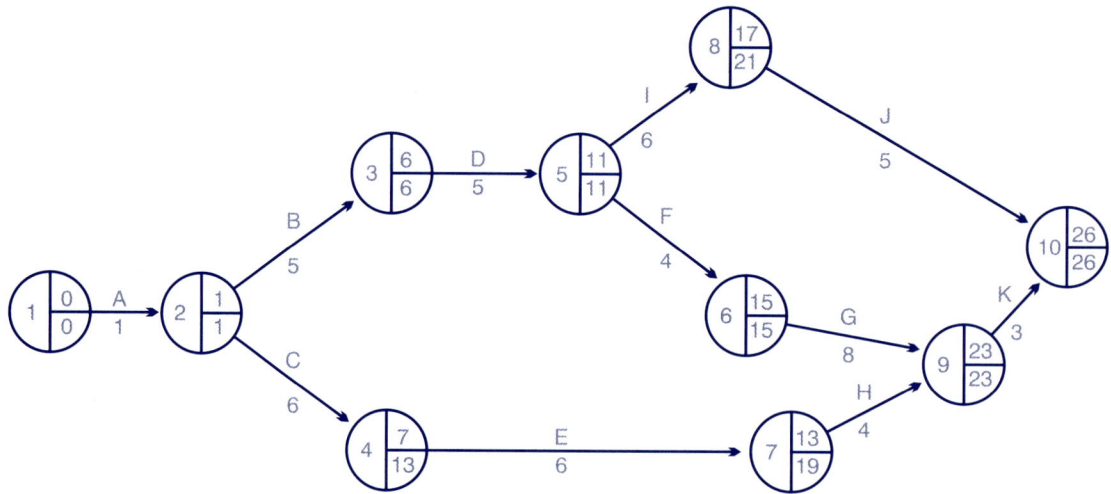

Compare your response with our commentary in Appendix 1.

03-2-9   Resource Analysis

So far we have looked at project planning as a time-based exercise, but for a project plan to be workable, it must analyse the requirement for resources across time, and devise the most available efficient allocation. Although it is usually practical to start the 'time plan' with an assumption that resources will be available as required, the plan then needs to be revisited to assess where resourcing is a constraint upon planned activity.

The critical resource on many projects is staffing. Here we will consider resource allocation primarily as the scheduling of staff to the project, but where other resources will have a critical influence (e.g. if equipment is on loan for a limited period, or if a project needs to generate cash to finance later activity) similar principles will apply.

The term 'loading' is used to describe the assignment of people to tasks. Not all people on a project are interchangeable — specialisms and limited availability will limit the extent to which available human resources can be assigned to critical activities. Human resource allocation therefore consists of a series of decisions about where and when the available team members will be most valuable to the project. The project manager has to steer a course between 'overload' (too many resources assigned to an activity) and 'underload' (too few assigned).

The rarely-struck balance will achieve a situation where:

Work required = Resource available

Resource Definition

Looking specifically at staffing, there are two ways in which the resource can be defined:

☞ The resources that are used continuously on an activity, e.g. activity M requires three people for its duration. An assumption is that resources are used at a constant rate.

☞ The amount of work required by an activity. This is usually given in staff-hours.

The latter gives a method of varying the duration of an activity. At its simplest, if the staffing is doubled it should halve the time. In practice this is rarely true. As the number of personnel is increased, efficiency should increase accordingly, but diminishing return means an optimum minimum time will be reached by which staff-hours will increase with increased manning. However, although the relationship between resource assignment and efficiency is not a linear one, it may be expedient for project managers to first work on the assumption that it is (they may subsequently build in factors relating to the 'quality' of the resources and the extent to which work can be parcelled out, but a catch-all statistical formula is likely to prove elusive!)

To say an activity is a fifty hour job could mean that fifty people could do it in one hour or one person in fifty hours. But a more likely situation is that it could be a fifty hour job when between three and eight people are employed.

There are some important practical points to bear in mind when planning resources. Most resources (particularly human) are not of equal ability. When applied to staffing, the tortuous efficiency equation has to account for differing experience, competences and attitudes; irregular availability must be borne in mind (holidays, sickness, 'downtime', etc.); and occasionally it may even be necessary to consider the quality of management!

All of this is compelling proof that the onus of achieving efficiency must not be placed entirely on planning activity — performance measurement and control have a crucial part to play in diagnosing inefficient performance and setting corrective action in train (this may involve revisiting the resource allocation plan but other, more direct, measures may be more appropriate).

Analysis of Resource Requirement

A convenient method of analysing a resource requirement is to prepare a Gantt or bar chart from the critical path diagram. From this a histogram of resource requirement can be prepared.

Consider first an earlier example of a critical path network.

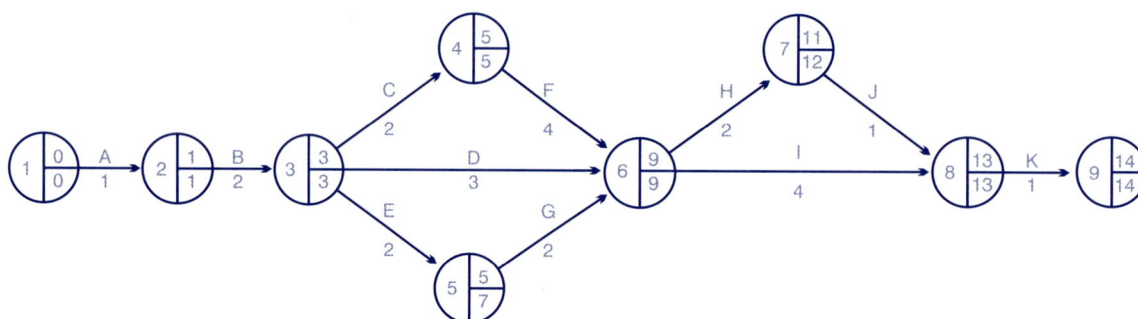

Below is the analysis table corresponding to this network diagram.

Activity	Duration	Resource	Early Start	Late Start	Early Finish	Late Finish	Float
A	1	1	0	0	1	1	0
B	2	1	1	1	3	3	0
C	2	3	3	3	5	5	0
D	3	2	3	6	6	9	3
E	2	1	3	5	5	7	2
F	4	2	5	5	9	9	0
G	2	1	5	7	7	9	2
H	2	1	9	10	11	12	1
I	4	1	9	9	13	13	0
J	1	2	11	12	12	13	1
K	1	1	13	13	14	14	0

From our network diagram and the analysis table above, the next step is to prepare charts which present the requirement for resources over the project term. The early and late start and finish columns are particularly useful for this.

On the following pages are two bar charts and two histograms, used to display the resource requirement for two scenarios (the earliest and latest possible starts). A simplified assumption has been made that each activity requires one team. More varied loading can be presented using these techniques and it is possible to differentiate between different types of resourcing (by colouring or shading for instance) — the final result would be more elaborate than in our illustrations.

Some points to note with this exercise are:

☞ It is normal to look at the two (early and late) extremes when looking at resource levels.

☞ Note the method of drawing the bar chart so that float on non-critical activities is shown.

☞ When all activities start as late as possible, the resources do not exceed five and appear more evenly spread.

☞ Often this plotting of extremes points to a compromise solution for resource allocation.

☞ Because of the great potential for variation in this exercise, it is better suited to computer modelling than manual preparation — most modern project management software contains resource analysis features.

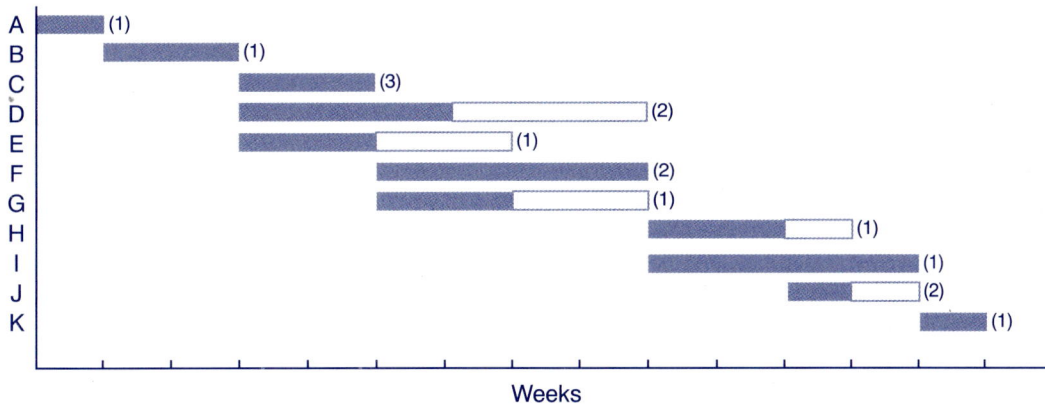

Weeks

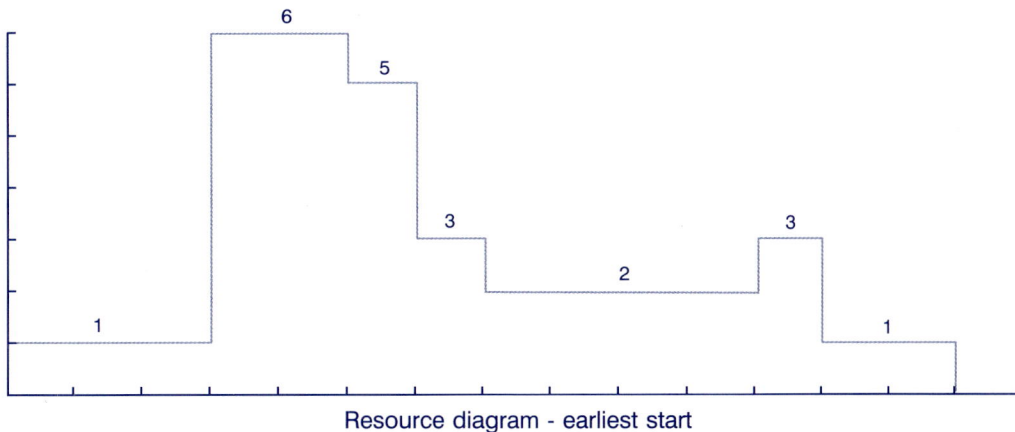

Resource diagram - earliest start

www.universal-manager.co.uk

Planning and Controlling Projects

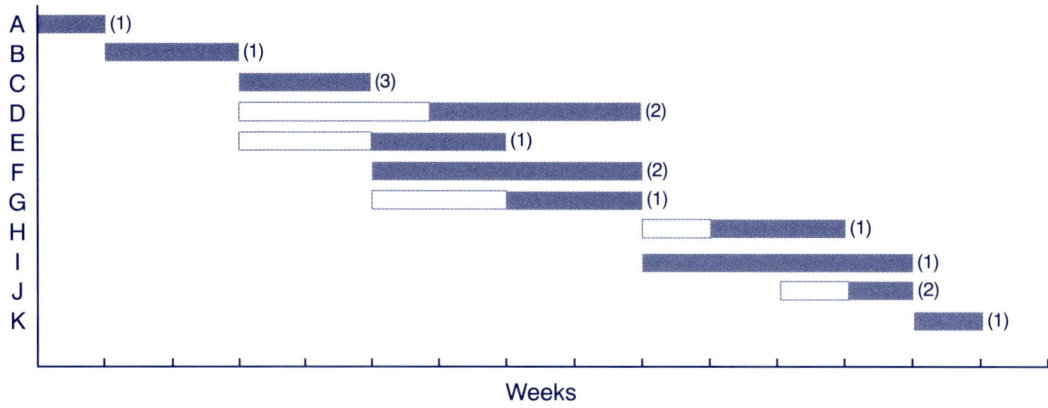

Weeks

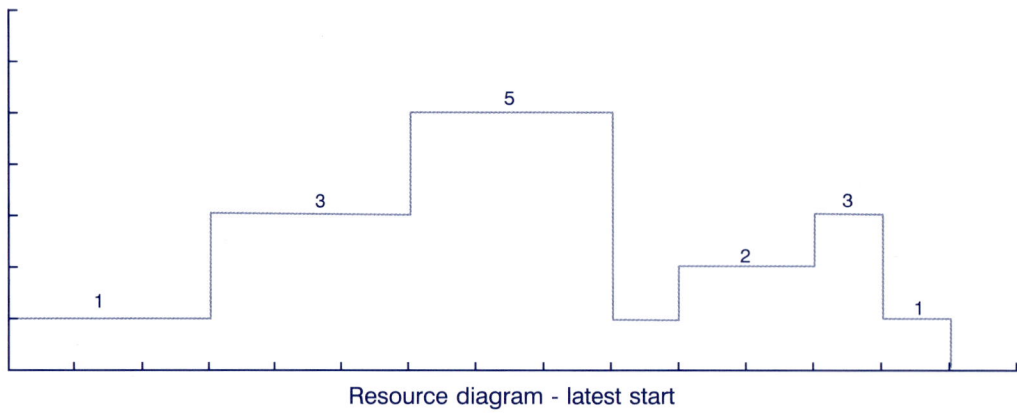

Resource diagram - latest start

![ACTION] **ACTIVITY 12**

The data tabulated below describes the activities in a project to create the engineering design for a new process plant. The project manager needs to carry out an analysis of the data to determine how long the project will take and the resources required. Times given are in weeks and the resources are individual people.

Description	Activity	Dependency	Duration	Resources
Equipment specs	A	—	3	2
P & I D	B	—	4	1
Foundation details	C	A	5	1
Piping Design	D	B	2	2
Civil Design	E	C	2	3
Piping CAD	F	C	6	1
Structural Design	G	E	2	3
Building Design	H	E	1	2
MTO	I	F,D	3	3
Structural Estimate	J	G	2	1
Building Estimate	K	H	2	1
Plant Estimate	L	I	1	1

(a)　Using the tabulated data prepare a:

- ☞ Critical Path Diagram
- ☞ Gantt chart
- ☞ Resource Histogram.

(b)　From your diagrams determine:

- ☞ The time required to complete the detailed design
- ☞ The critical path
- ☞ The maximum resources required at any time
- ☞ The week in which the resources are at a maximum.

Compare your answers with our commentary in Appendix 1.

03-2-10 Activity on Node Networking

In AoN networking, the node represents the activity and the arrow represents the dependency. The node is represented by a rectangle. Many of the principles and logic are not unlike Activity on Arrow and it is not necessary to spend so much time to obtain an understanding.

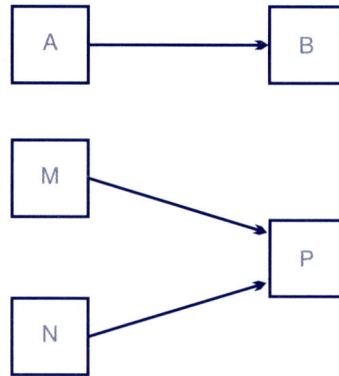

Activity P depends on activity M and activity N

A number of key conventions are different with the AoN approach:

- There are no dummy activities in activity on node networks
- Duration is usually, but not always, included in the node
- The time that must elapse between the start of one activity and the start of the next is added to the dependency arrow
- Usually, this time requirement and the duration will be the same but where an activity can start before the end of a preceding activity (on which it is dependent), the figures can be different.

For straightforward networks where all activities cannot start until dependent activities are complete, the duration need not be stated on the node. Here are some ways of presenting the node:

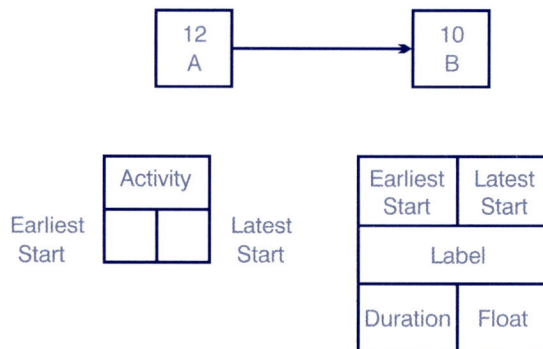

The last shown method of representing is compliant with British Standard BS 4335 1987.

The start of a project begins with a node of zero duration. All opening activities emerge from this node. The finish of a project ends with a node and all finishing activities come together at this node.

Calculating Total Project Time

The details below illustrate basic steps in a project to overhaul a Reactor system (the nature of the project and its activities are not significant for the following exercises).

Task	Description	Duration	Dependency
A	Shut down	1	—
B	Steam Reactor	2	A
C	Steam Column	1	A
D	Open Reactor/Close	3	B
E	Open Column	1	C
F	Renew Support	4	E
G	Replace Packing	1	F
H	Repair Steam Main	5	B,C
I	Steam Catalyst	1	D,H

The Forward Pass

We will use the second of the methods shown for representing the nodes for this network, and will show the duration times on the arrows.

We begin with a 'start node' and assign an earliest start time of 0 to it. Proceed to each activity in turn and calculate the EST from the preceding activity and dependency time. As with Activity on Arrow networks, where an activity depends on more than one activity, the longest time is taken. The process is carried out until the 'finish node' is reached to give the Earliest Start Time for the finish (in other words the Finish Time.) This gives us a figure for total project time which we put into both the Earliest Start and Latest Start boxes on the finish node.

The Backward Pass

The critical path is obtained by carrying out a backward pass and working out the Latest Start Time. Start with the finish node and. taking the Finish Time subtract the duration to give the Latest Start Times. Where two activities emerge from one activity, the shorter time is selected. The critical path lies along those activities where the Earliest Start Times and the Latest Start Times are the same.

Planning and Controlling Projects

Float

In the Activity on Node network, the total float is given by the difference between the Latest Start Time and the Earliest Start Time. The critical path is the one with no float.

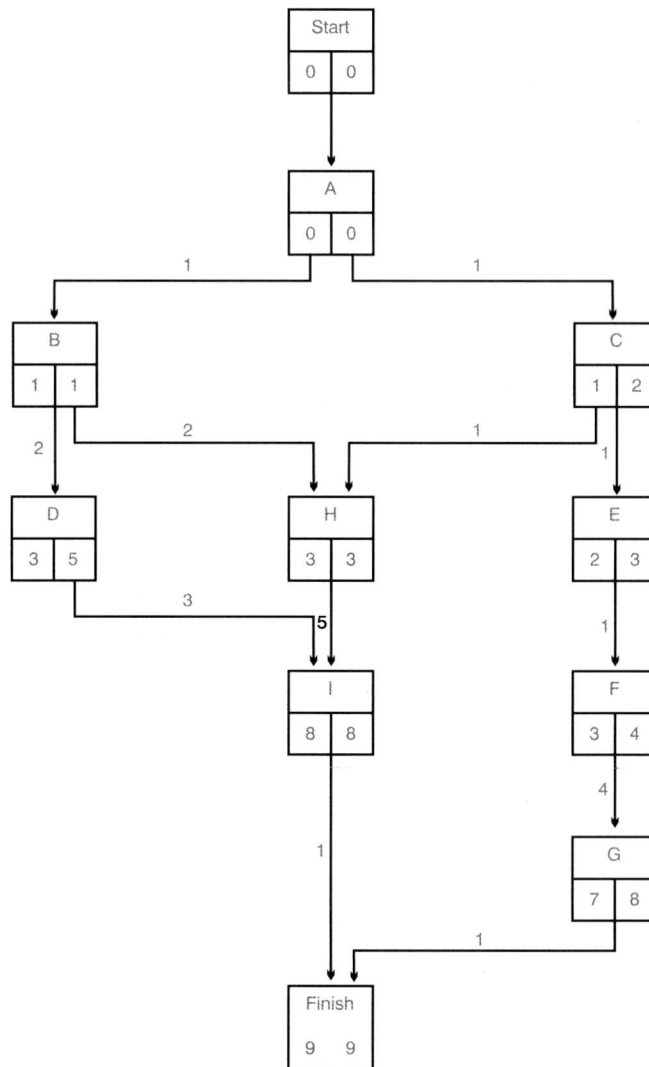

Although the above network diagram is shown in portrait, it would be more usual to have larger diagrams set out in landscape on project management software.

03-3 IMPLEMENTATION AND CONTROL

03-3

03-3 IMPLEMENTATION AND CONTROL

Many project management practitioners and theorists consider planning to be the hub of the discipline, and with good reason — the systematic planning methods outlined in the previous section enable the project manager to rationalize a scale and complexity of activity which would not otherwise be manageable. All subsequent activity should therefore be performed and controlled with close reference to the documents generated during the planning stage.

But the planning stage does not end with the production of elaborate charts and diagrams showing the shortest possible critical path, or the most efficient possible use of resources. These are visual aids which, while they may be a great source of pride and comfort to the project manager, will not on their own be greatly useful to the other parties involved (the client, some stakeholders, some project team members). From the WBS, the Gantt charts and the CPA diagrams, a secondary layer of information needs to be developed which will have more direct relevance to the various project players.

This section considers various formats for providing project information, and goes on to link these to project monitoring.

03-3-1 Working to the Plan

.A project's plan provides the basis for implementation and control. It defines the scope and the objectives of the project, and specifies the project's structure, organization, resource allocation and schedule. Therefore, as a physical product, the plan will integrate several components, probably into a single document, but which will have more than one version. Variance between different versions of the plan will be a function of:

☛ Varying information needs of recipients
☛ Revisions to the plan over time.

In order to gain commitment from the full project team, it is advisable to involve them in preparation of the plan: this should help to ensure that it becomes a working document, constantly consulted and updated in line with actual developments.

It is not unknown in the world of projects for the plan to be a huge and intimidating document, cast into the project manager's bottom drawer, and never referred to at all during project implementation. Reiss reports on a project in his experience where the only time the plan saw daylight was when the client visited!

CASE STUDY

In Exxon the key document for project management is the *Project Execution Plan*. This covers all aspects of a project in summary and will reference other documents such as:

☞ The contracting plan
☞ Design documentation
☞ Insurance policies
☞ Controls plan.

It is common practice to distinguish between different versions of the project plan. A key distinction is between the 'summary plan' and the 'detailed plan'. The summary plan is to be shared with the client and internal stakeholders such as the senior management team or company board. It needs to provide a level of information to enable detection of significant variation from the project's budget and schedule, and to support strategic decision-making. Typically therefore, it will contain a mix of strategic and tactical information including:

☞ The project definition (purpose, objectives, people, end results, standards, scope and strategy)
☞ The breakdown of major parts of the project and their associated work packages
☞ Summary of risks and associated strategies
☞ An outline schedule with milestones and deliverables
☞ Budgetary information.

The detailed plan will build upon the summary by providing operational information required by the project team. Key additional ingredients will include:

- Responsibility matrix
- Full schedule with key events and review points
- Categorization of project risks and their associated response options
- Standard operating procedures for the project (this might cover standard terminology, purchasing procedures and change request procedures)
- Budgetary information
- The critical path analysis.

The last two may appear to provide the most crucial information for project team members since they set the required standards for resource control and completion of activities. In fact it is a matter of some debate whether these essentially management information items should be shared with team members (including contractors and sub-contractors).

ACTIVITY 13

What arguments might there be against providing budgetary information and critical path print-outs to project team members?

Compare your response with our commentary in Appendix 1.

In the end this is a matter for the project manager's discretion — a balanced approach will motivate the team to improve upon planned performance levels without overburdening them with information.

03-3-2   Project Communication

Effective communication on projects is about making sure all participants get the information they need, in a form they can use, and at appropriate times. The effective project manager will make judicious use of all the available forms of communication:

- Human contact
- Paper
- Electronic.

Contact with other people takes place at structured meetings and interviews and via less formal conversations. In all of these contacts, the project manager is expected to be better informed than those he is dealing with, and to be able to respond to their diverse needs. This requires time for preparation prior to meetings and other contacts, a clear grasp of the divergent interests of key players on the project, a certain flair for diplomatic presentation, and an ability to ask the right questions (when aspects of a project are not going to plan, it is unusual for the real causes to be immediately identified and volunteered by those responsible).

Even in this computer age, projects can generate a rainforest of paperwork. Filing systems need to be sufficiently robust and well-organized to deal with multiple versions of the same documents (the project plan, proposals, responsibility matrices, etc.) as well as the usual welter of letters, memos, minutes of meetings, reports, and so on. With design-oriented projects (such as software developments or construction projects), control of key documents whether drawings, storyboards, asset lists or specifications, is especially important.

A later part of this section is devoted entirely to a discussion of the uses of software and communication technologies in project management. What follows is a summary of various non-electronic communication methods available to the project manager.

Meetings

Project meetings

Project meetings are an essential part of the project management operation. At the implementation stage and afterwards there is likely to be a variety of meetings scheduled to review progress, refine or roll out plans and to communicate decisions.

Depending on project size and duration these may be of the order of once a week, once a month or tagged to specific project milestones.

Although project meetings will vary as to their purpose, frequency and attendance they will nearly all share the aim of taking decisions about:

- ☞ The action to be taken
- ☞ Responsibility for that action.

Generally, the questions a project meeting should address are also similar, regardless of context or attendance:

- ☞ Where are we against the plan?
- ☞ What can we do to eliminate or minimize variances from the plan?
- ☞ How reliable is our evidence of non-variance?

The check point review

This is held when a milestone has occurred. Usually a high level meeting to update senior players including the client, a check point review will discuss major issues and decisions such as whether to proceed, whether deliverables are of the required standard, and even whether the project should be terminated. Typical attendees would be the project manager, a senior client representative, a senior management representative and the most influential internal and external stakeholders.

The status review

This is regular meeting to discuss the nuts and bolts of the project. Standing agenda items will include project progress, performance and variance from schedule and budget, and quality issues. This is an appropriate forum for a project manager to receive structured reports from the team, qualitative feedback on successes and problems, and is also appropriate for policy announcements (such as significant changes, new operating procedures, etc.).

Though the format should be carefully structured to ensure full coverage of critical performance matters, these meetings work best when there is room for free ranging discussion, so that project team members are encouraged to share ideas and information. The status review is attended by team leaders and client representatives and is chaired by the project manager.

Like the other meetings described, this type of review will focus on comparing actual with planned progress, and on testing the reliability of on-target reports.

Detailed minutes are particularly important here, and the project manager must clearly communicate the actions required of the contractor whilst ensuring that cost implications of these actions are spelled out.

Independent reviews

With high risk projects it is common to involve independent 'experts' in project reviews, particularly before critical decisions (i.e. at project 'gates'). These 'experts' may be technical or subject specialists, or they could constitute a sample intended to reflect the profile of the project's end users. For instance, a new software program will be *tested* to destruction by internal specialists, but will also be *piloted* with users. (The distinct purposes of the test and pilot exercises must be clearly identified.) Of course, a meeting is not the only method by which expert reviews can be undertaken, but it can provide a useful means of:

☞ Highlighting critical feedback and eliminating unsubstantiated or unimportant views
☞ Enriching the quality of feedback.

03-3

The staff meeting

This is an optional communication format at which no senior staff are present. It may be held regularly but probably not often — bi-monthly or quarterly. The ostensible purpose is for the project manager to make policy announcements, and to air significant operational issues, but it may serve other (less publicized) ends:

☞ As an opportunity for the project team to spend uninterrupted time attempting to solve serious operational problems
☞ As a 'no blame' session where team members are able to 'confess' errors, ask 'stupid questions' and identify operational problems.

Ad hoc meetings

Although conforming to no specific communication schedule, and with no definable attendance, these are often the meetings at which significant issues are raised and frequently resolved. In essence this is because the *ad hoc* meeting arises for a specific purpose, and has a self-selecting attendance. The ideal *ad hoc* meeting provides a few uninterrupted hours in which those involved may tackle a burning project issue. However, the obvious danger is that the *ad hoc* meeting will become a habitual format, leaned upon by project participants who cannot achieve their objectives alone.

There is an inclination, particularly in the small business, to avoid:

☞ Too many meetings
☞ Unplanned meetings.

This reluctance to waste everybody's time in unstructured, unproductive talking is understandable but it can have the unwanted effect that contributors to a project (particularly at staff level) feel unable to communicate on matters relating to project performance.

ACTIVITY 14

Describe one or two project meeting formats in place within your organization. Assess the success of each format in terms of:

☞   Focussing contributors on issues critical to project success
☞   Encouraging clear, honest reporting on progress
☞   Enabling all attendees to contribute.

Now read on.

Reports

Project reports are an essential way of keeping everyone informed: if the report format is well structured it should force both writer and reader to think about project-critical issues, to identify variances from planned performance and identify options for corrective action. Some features of a typical project reporting format for team members are as follows:

- Produced at regular intervals, say monthly
- Primary audience will be the project manager, who may edit reports before they go to the client, senior management, etc.
- Forms a history of the project
- Accent on factual and quantitative information, especially time, expenditure, measured quality and barriers
- Standardized, and probably computerized to speed preparation, collation and assimilation.

03-3

Elements which would be expected in a typical project report will include:

- Project title (and number)
- Executive summary (possibly narrative)
- Bar chart showing actual against planned progress
- Comparison of actual versus planned expenditure and resource consumption
- Summary of cost situation
- Summary of project progress
- Analysis of key current project risks.

Two of the most useful documents in contract reporting are the **bar chart** showing actual versus predicted progress and the **spend curve** showing a graph of predicted expenditure against actual, both at the date of reporting. The main advantage of these is that they are readily understandable by the non-specialist. The two formats do have certain shortcomings however, and we will discuss these later in this section.

Correspondence

Projects accumulate large amounts of correspondence, whether paper-based or electronic — it is usually advisable that all contact between sponsor and project team, project manager and sub-contractor are officially recorded and stored, even if it is just a case of making brief notes after a telephone conversation. The consequences of not keeping a formal record, even of what may appear spontaneous verbal contact, can provide a hard lesson for the unwary project manager.

As with reports, correspondence will provide a project history, invaluable for handovers, final reviews, or tracing the background to problems.   This dossier is not the place to detail processes for efficient storage and retrieval of correspondence and other project paperwork, but there are one or two actions a project manager is recommended to take:

- ☞ Devise or buy in a simple storage and retrieval system at an early stage (probably during the planning process — when it may provide a welcome diversion!)
- ☞ Part of the system should be to make clear distinctions between different types of document, and different versions of documents
- ☞ Introduce the system to team members as one of the standard operating procedures
- ☞ Ensure team members apply the system (a good-natured but effective approach might be to 'fine' team members who are guilty of not using the system)
- ☞ 'Weed' files periodically (this task too can have certain therapeutic qualities).

03-3-3   The Impact of Information Technology

Virtually all operational processes within organizations have been revolutionized over the past twenty years by the rapid developments in Information and Communications Technology (ICT).   From the introduction of the personal computer, through the explosion of productivity-oriented software, to the more recent expansion of networking capacity, the way we work has been transformed — and project management is right at the centre of this shift from manual to computer-based operations.   In this part of the dossier, we will look at two aspects of developing ICT which have direct relevance to the management of projects:

- ☞ Project management software
- ☞ Network systems.

Project Management Software

There is an enormous variety of available project management software products. It is not the intention of this dossier to evaluate them or to recommend specific systems (advice of this sort can be found in specialist project management periodicals such as *Project Manager Today* and very often in computer magazines). However, we will attempt to provide sufficient understanding of the capabilities and requirements of project management software to guide selection and implementation of appropriate system(s). First, we should establish the basics.

PAUSE TO REFLECT

(a)   What do you think project management software does?

(b)   Why would anyone need project management software?

Now read on.

Whatever extravagant claims manufacturers make about the features and presentation formats offered by their competing packages, the essential function of project management software is to 'model' data relating to a project's time and resources. Most current packages will automate preparation and presentation of the various planning tools described in section 03-2 (the bar and Gantt charts, PERT and critical path analysis, resource analysis and assignment, etc.). The advantages of computerized over manual methods are evident. Software can:

- ☛ Store and present huge amounts of data
- ☛ Assimilate and process critical adjustments to plans
- ☛ Manipulate data for presentation from multiple perspectives
- ☛ Quickly process and display alternative courses of action.

It follows that the need for project management software within an organization will depend on the extent to which its projects are large, complex, multiple and interdependent. In fact, any project which involves more than a handful of people, and which contains uncertainty over optimum timing and resource-loading, will benefit from the application of project management software.

Planning and Controlling Projects

It is possible to identify two main types of software according to their application:

Standalone. Typically installed on a single computer, this type of software enables individual users to automate planning on individual projects — information tends to be shared via print-outs. Common examples are Microsoft Project and Timeline. The price range is approximately between £80 and £2,000 although more expensive packages are available.

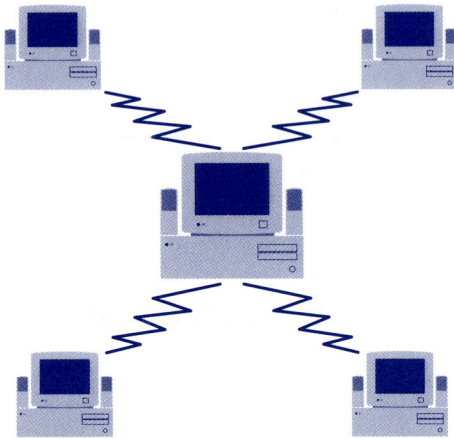

Multi-user. Networkable versions of standalone products are often available, but the true multi-user system is a far more powerful beast with a central processor which stores and processes data fed in at numerous satellite terminals. This type of software is geared towards large organizations managing complex programmes — carefully worked out authorization protocols will dictate the extent to which satellite users can enter and modify individual project plans, while the central processor will tend to be run by one or more specialist planners. Prominent among manufacturers of multi-user software are Lucas, Innate and Mantix. A custom-built model with multiple user licenses can easily come out at £30,000 or more.

Choosing the Right Package

Many project management textbooks contain advice on specifying project management software (Lock and Reiss are particularly helpful in this regard).

ACTIVITY 15

What follows is a distillation of some of the best advice on software selection. If you or your organization are planning to purchase a project management package, you may find this checklist helpful.

(a)   What operating system does it run on?

(b)   Is it compatible with other software in the organization? And with peripherals such as printers?

(c)   Will it run on your network?

www.universal-manager.co.uk

(d)   Is it easy to use in terms of:
  - ☞   Level of specialist planning or programming knowledge required
  - ☞   Level of on-screen and paper-based support provided
  - ☞   Complexity of screen layout and menus?

(e)   Is training provided? If so, in what format (personal delivery, CD-ROM, manual, etc.)?

(f)   Could it cope with double the number of projects currently managed by your organization?

(g)   Can it integrate and consolidate data from multiple projects?

(h)   Can it cope easily with the numbers of activities and linkages in the largest and most complex of your organization's current projects?

(i)   What reporting formats are available?

(j)   Can it analyse and load resources? Will resource features tie in with the kinds of resource managed in your projects?

(k)   Can the program analyse and assign costs according to the criteria used in your projects?

(l)   Can users test possible adjustments through 'what-if' scenarios?

(m)   Does it have the capacity to cross-assign codes to activities, resources and costs?

(n)   What security devices does the programme contain?

(o)   What are the licensing, maintenance and support arrangements for the software?

(p)   What is the package's track record:
  - ☞   Has it been refined through generations
  - ☞   Who else uses it?

Now read on.

Implementing Project Management Software

For every satisfied user there are probably another four disillusioned souls with a poor opinion of project management software. The most commonly heard complaint is that the output from the software (reports, and graphic displays of time, cost and resource arrangements) is meagre in relation to the input (specification, purchase, training, data input and manipulation). The critics do have a point — there is a lot of work to be done to get the optimum return from the right package — but they tend to be users who have:

- ☛ Either selected the wrong package
- ☛ Or failed to grasp or exploit the full capacity of the software
- ☛ Or given up on the software before reaching the 'payback zone'.

The payback zone is that happy state where the project team is confidently using the software to analyse time and resource requirements, plan activity and resourcing, try out alternative scenarios, track and report on project performance, control budgets and timekeeping, and so on. Project management software pays when it is used to communicate, to inform decision-making and to monitor progress.

Getting to that point can in itself constitute a project which we can divide into four stages as shown in the illustration on the next page.

www.universal-manager.co.uk

Implementing Project Management Software

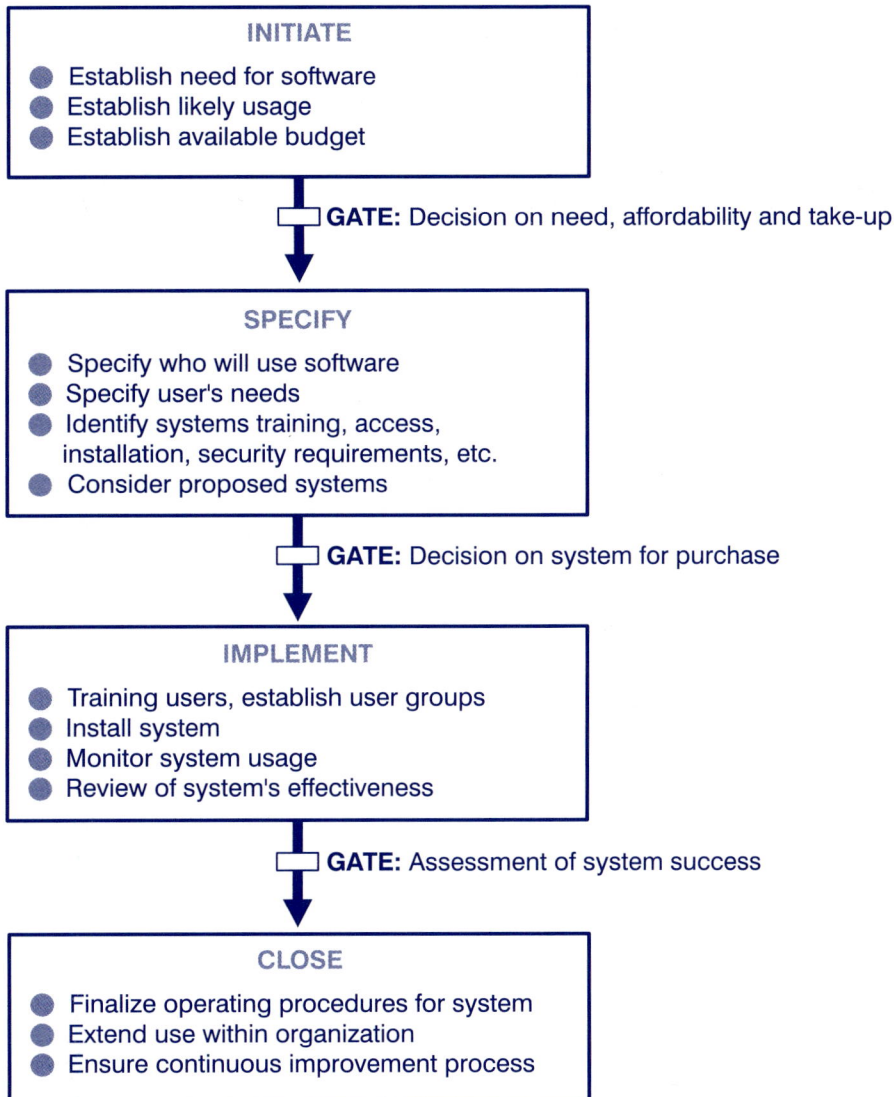

```
┌──────────────────────────────────────────┐
│                 INITIATE                   │
│  ● Establish need for software             │
│  ● Establish likely usage                  │
│  ● Establish available budget              │
└──────────────────────────────────────────┘
        │
        │  GATE: Decision on need, affordability and take-up
        ▼
┌──────────────────────────────────────────┐
│                 SPECIFY                    │
│  ● Specify who will use software           │
│  ● Specify user's needs                    │
│  ● Identify systems training, access,      │
│    installation, security requirements, etc.│
│  ● Consider proposed systems               │
└──────────────────────────────────────────┘
        │
        │  GATE: Decision on system for purchase
        ▼
┌──────────────────────────────────────────┐
│                IMPLEMENT                   │
│  ● Training users, establish user groups   │
│  ● Install system                          │
│  ● Monitor system usage                    │
│  ● Review of system's effectiveness        │
└──────────────────────────────────────────┘
        │
        │  GATE: Assessment of system success
        ▼
┌──────────────────────────────────────────┐
│                  CLOSE                     │
│  ● Finalize operating procedures for system│
│  ● Extend use within organization          │
│  ● Ensure continuous improvement process   │
└──────────────────────────────────────────┘
```

03-3

The project stages illustrated could be refined or developed, particularly for purchasers of elaborate multi-user systems: for instance the 'specify' stage might include a limited trial before full implementation of the software. But whatever the scale of investment, the overriding priorities will be to establish a system which:

☛ Is affordable
☛ Can be used with confidence by everyone who needs to use it
☛ Will produce the outputs desired by your organization.

Lientz and Rea describe project management software as a 'political tool' — it is an apt description with different layers of meaning. Firstly, as a modelling tool, the software can be used to present several alternative pictures of current and predicted reality — the political project manager will be adept at selecting the picture which best suits his own ends, whether this means impressing the client with a detailed level of planning, or filtering data to focus on a specific scenario (such as the deployment of a specific resource or the dependency on a particular task). Secondly, once implemented, there can be a tendency to treat every output of the project management software as gospel — in extreme situations projects can be paralysed by this dependence on the software, to the extent where no decision is made without consulting this electronic guru. The flipside of this attitude can occur in organizations where the prevailing attitude (particularly at senior levels) is anti-technology — in such an environment, a project manager who spends too much time with the software may be condemned as a nerd, out of touch with the practicalities of projects and day-to-day work.

Network Systems

By 'network systems' we mean any IT system which links two or more computers — this definition encompasses local area networks and wide area networks (LANs and WANs), the internet and intranets — and we also refer to those tools which rely on linked computers, such as video-conferencing and virtual teamworking.

The two essential benefits offered by these systems and tools are:

- Enhanced communication capacity (also facilitated by related innovations in portable PCs and mobile telephones)
- The ability to pool knowledge.

Any project where the team is 'fractured' or dispersed has much to gain from these ever improving technologies.

CASE STUDY

Ghosh and Bartlett (1998) relay the experience of the McKinsey management consultancy when faced with delivering a project in challenging circumstances:

☞ The job was to bid for a study to develop a financial services strategy for a major Australian corporation

☞ The most suitable in-house subject expert was based in Boston, USA and was not available for the first six weeks of the assignment; other identified experts were similarly remote (based in London, New York and Paris)

☞ The local, Australian, project team did not have sufficient expertise in financial services

☞ The team had a short time to deliver for a highly demanding client.

03-3

The fact that the project was eventually successful can be, in part, attributed to the 'edge' supplied by McKinsey's excellent ICT systems:

☞ The local project team had access to a vast knowledge bank — networked databases containing records of all proposals, reports, lessons and associated information derived from all of the company's previous work, worldwide. From their initial trawl the 'non-expert' team was able to generate 42 pertinent ideas.

☞ Dispersal of the total project team across several time zones effectively enabled 24-hour working on the project. When the local team hit a snag, they could e-mail USA or Europe and have someone working on it 'overnight'.

PAUSE TO REFLECT

What specific applications might network technologies have to the projects managed by your organization?

Now read on.

Planning and Controlling Projects

The extent to which network technologies can support and enhance project management in your organization will depend largely on the extent to which:

- ☛ Projects involve large teams
- ☛ Projects are delivered by dispersed or fractured teams
- ☛ Projects require collaborative effort
- ☛ Different projects inter-link (e.g. resource sharing between projects)
- ☛ Project outputs are capable of on-screen presentation (web or multimedia development projects are ideal in this respect).

Here are five practical ways in which network technologies can benefit project management:

(a) *E-mail* can speed up communication between project participants, and the ability to attach documents makes it an excellent medium for sharing information on plans, progress and budgets.

(b) *Mobile communications* such as laptop computers and cellphones make key people more productive: they are contactable when away from the project centre and able to work in what would otherwise be idle time (travelling, overnight stays, etc.)

(c) The use of *groupware* gives asynchronous access for project team members to the same computer applications, and the same files. A relatively recent development in this field is virtual team working which allows dispersed team members to exchange information, to 'meet' and review key documents, and to vote on preferences. It also provides the more familiar chat and conferencing facilities.

(d) *Networked databases* provide fast, multiple access to information. Many companies now network customer databases containing all customer details, contact histories and market profiling capabilities. At their simplest, such systems function by enabling team members to access customer records quickly in response to requests and enquiries — for extra 'edge' they can be linked to telephone systems so that a customer call will prompt the database automatically to find the relevant record. Some of the problems surrounding Internet searches can also be addressed by creating and networking in-house databases — typically, project team members who find useful information on the world wide web will paste it into the networked database, thus developing an in-house knowledge bank.

84

(e) *Video-conferencing* still has its drawbacks: dependence on links at both ends, and variable quality in the transmission of sound and images are two. But where the right conditions exist it can provide an effective meeting format: body language is visible, documents can be exchanged and annotated, and paradoxically, where the link is of poor quality, this can contribute to sharpening the focus of the meeting and prompt the participants to establish formal or informal protocols for speaking, listening, interjecting, assenting, etc.

I think he means 'No'!

03-3-4   Monitoring Activity

Controlling the use of time and resources on a project is, for the most part, a monitoring activity. The main focus of project monitoring will be the schedule.

The Schedule

The schedule sets out how long each individual part of the project will take, who is accountable, and possibly which resources are associated with it (alternatively, resources may be tracked separately via budgetary or resource analysis formats). The essential information on a schedule will be:

- Key deliverables linked to
- Key review dates.

The project manager is responsible for getting commitment to the schedule, tracking it and refining it over time. It is crucial to have a clear, complete and accurate schedule: this sets the course for the entire project — it is likely to be the most consulted aspect of the project plan.

Monitoring project performance is therefore largely about tracking progress against the schedule, and identifying variances. Variances can occur for any number of reasons (many of which are outside the control of the project manager), so the firmness of project control will rest heavily on the project manager's ability to pick up variation early, to spot unfavourable trends and select and initiate appropriate corrective action. The schedule is a living document which may require re-forecasting, chasing through to end dates, and corresponding changes to resource allocation.

Data Collection

The most reliable way to obtain consistent data is by the use of standard reporting procedures. Every organization has its own particular format, developed to suit the type of project being handled. The main areas for comparison will be:

- Time spent
- Key times (mainly task starts and finishes)
- Money
- Cash flow
- Material and equipment purchases
- Productivity (how much work for how many hours).

Update

There are many forms, produced by a variety of disciplines, used for reporting. A key one reports dates for different tasks. This could have headings something like the following:

Form G/99B

Task No.	Description	Accountable	Plan Start	Plan Finish	Actual Start	Actual Finish	Modified Start	Modified Finish

www.universal-manager.co.uk

Whereas in the above report the planned and actual data will be precise, the more important modified data will be predicted and therefore partly subjective. Significant modifications need to be fed back into the project plan — a revised critical path, and modified resource loading may result. Another approach is to require the project contributors to estimate percentage completion of their activities — this tends to be a subjective exercise, with rather optimistic estimates until the day of reckoning draws near. However, some aspects of progress can be measured exactly: e.g. percentage of a construction completed, number of sections of a book or software programme designed, etc.

Similar charts to the one illustrated on the previous page can be devised to track:

03-3

☛ Hours spent on project activities (some operations will have standard time sheets)
☛ Materials consumed
☛ Equipment purchases.

Summary descriptions of various other available formats follow.

Progress Bar Chart

Typically this type of monitoring format would have columns for:

☛ Task number
☛ Description
☛ Accountability
☛ Scheduled start
☛ Scheduled finish.

The last, wider column, is used for the bar chart, with bars for 'planned progress' , 'critical factors' , 'non-critical factors' , 'work in progress' and 'completed work'. Planned and completed milestones may also be marked on the chart.

Deliverable Report

This is a table showing columns which can be labelled:

☞ Task description
☞ Accountable
☞ Planned finish
☞ Forecast finish
☞ Review by
☞ Accepted by
☞ Comments.

Management Summary

This can be a simplified version of the progress report form, restricted to presentation of scheduled start finish dates, accompanied by a basic bar chart showing planned and actual progress for each activity (or work stage if a purely strategic overview is required).

Milestone Report

In addition to the standard first three columns showing 'planned finish', 'forecast finish' and 'actual finish', this report will contain a column for comment on any milestones that have slipped ('slippage'). It highlights work which is likely to be late, so that the project manager can assess the requirement for corrective action.

Some of the most useful information for the project manager is not quantifiable. In the monitoring process the project manger collects feedback or information from wherever he can. Much of it is obtained informally by enquiry (via both formal and informal contact with team members).

At scheduled meetings with team members, the project manager is looking for a verbal report (probably summarized in a written format). It is crucial for the project manager to be well-prepared for these meetings, fully familiar with progress to date, and with a clear idea of the abilities of team members and of the challenges they face. A useful tactic can be to encourage team members to take the lead in outlining progress and performance issues, freeing the project manager to listen, observe and question where appropriate.

PAUSE TO REFLECT

What, in your opinion, are the pros and cons of adopting a confrontational approach at this type of meeting?

Now read on.

The arguments here are similar in nature to the classic comparison of democratic and autocratic styles of management. Faced with a confrontational project manager, relatively few team members will rise to the occasion, and though the tone set will probably encourage the team to be well prepared and crisp at progress reviews, it may equally encourage them to conceal bad news. A challenging, sceptical undertone in performance reviews is not unhealthy, promoting accuracy and flexibility, but a project manager can ill afford to terrify the team into reluctant and incomplete reporting.

03-3

A more constructive technique for verifying the accuracy of information is 'review by presence'. This is where tangible evidence is required in support of reported facts. Effective project managers are as concerned with the quality of results as with the performance against schedule and budget. A project that is ahead of schedule or under budget may well be so because it has not met the required quality criteria. Performance reporting which prizes quality, may require supplementary evidence in the form of physical samples or demonstrations; quality inspection reports may be requested. Time will constrain the ability to carry out full quality assessments, but the verbal and written formats may be augmented by more direct monitoring action.

key point

Management by Walkabout

Management by walkabout or MBWA is one way of getting reliable information. This involves visiting offices or sites where the project is taking shape or where members of the team are likely to be. Permission may sometimes be required — this need not be an issue where MBWA is not adopted primarily as a surprise tactic, but rather as a genuine attempt to view the condition of ongoing work and to reinforce the presence of the project manager.

key point

In a fabrication project there is a great deal to be found out and the information cannot be easily doctored. It will be evident, for instance, if manufacture has not started, or if it is not as advanced as claimed. Activity or lack of it will be obvious, especially if the visit is unannounced. The same is true of building projects which have reached the implementation phase.

A significant advantage of MBWA is that there is no information filter between the facts at issue and the project manager. The only potential for faulty perception comes from the project manager's faculties, or from a failure to ask the right questions or inspect the right processes.

📁 03-3-5   Controlling Costs

Cost and time control tend to be carried out in parallel for projects. Many of the formats used for cost control are similar to those described for monitoring project time, with a similar focus on identifying variance.

The S-Curve

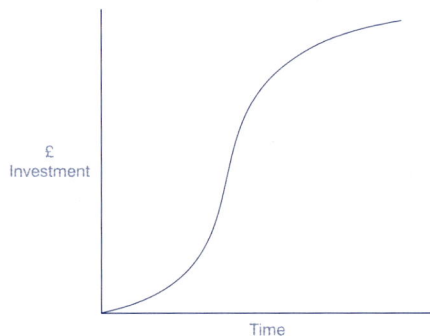

A recognized method of reporting data such as cumulative project costs, but which is also applicable to time (cumulative hours), is the S-curve — this plots cumulative total expenditure against time. Actual expenditure may be superimposed on forecast.

One of the problems with this type of monitoring is that there may be valid reasons for the actual not corresponding with the planned (for example, a major piece of equipment may be purchased early to obtain a discount). In the same way, lower spending is not necessarily a good sign — it could indicate that the project is running late. Even a direct match between actual and forecast patterns is no guarantee that everything is right. On a complex multi-package project, the overall summary S-curve rarely provides useful information. It is necessary to look beyond the summary at what is actually happening within each of the key components. The S-curve is a prompt for further investigation, and doesn't answer the essential questions:

- ☞ What have we achieved so far compared to what we should have achieved?
- ☞ How do the actual costs compare with the planned costs?
- ☞ What will be the effect on the final project?

Since monitoring is about comparison, other types of graphical representation are also used extensively. Gantt, bar and pie charts are all useful here — as is the histogram format.

Milestone Monitoring

This method overcomes some of the disadvantages of the simple S-curve. Since milestones are significant events, which relate to completion of packages, they are normally easy to present in relation to overall project progress. The dates on which they are due to be completed are known, as are the budgeted costs for the work leading up to them.

If the milestones with their associated costs are plotted as points on a time – cumulative cost curve (similar to the S-curve) the resulting information can be more meaningful. Budget data will be exactly as derived and there will be accurate information on the times of milestone achievement and the costs incurred.

03-3

In the ideal scenario, the planned and achieved milestone co-ordinates will coincide. For closer monitoring, separate graphs can be plotted for individual departments as well as a composite graphic display for the project.

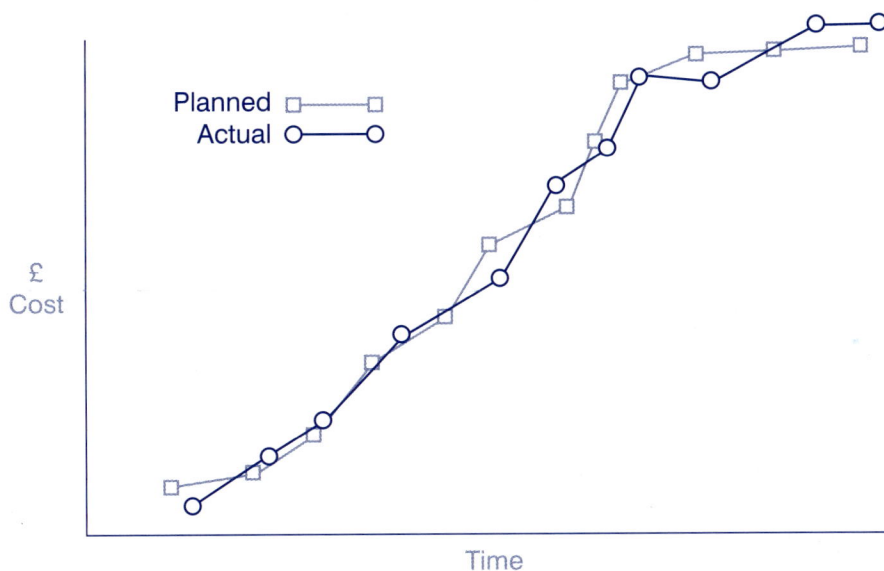

Certain deductions can be made from milestone monitoring. For example, if the milestones are late but the expenditure is less than budgeted, an evident option would be to spend more in order to bring the schedule back on course. If on the other hand expenditure is on budget but milestones are late, this would provide a warning that overspend was a serious possibility.

The disadvantage of milestone monitoring is that it deals with events that have already taken place — if things have gone wrong, the scope for correction is probably limited. The process does not contribute to monitoring work in progress, and in practice, predictions of final outcome based on milestone monitoring tend not to be very reliable. A method that tries to overcome these disadvantages is 'Earned Value' analysis.

Planning and Controlling Projects

Earned Value

A difficult relationship to establish in project monitoring, but an important one, is that between the actual work done and the time spent doing it, i.e. between physical achievement and financial or man-hour spend. 'Earned value' is a technique that attempts to measure this. It is particularly pertinent for 'failing' projects — behind schedule but ahead on spend.

A project contains budgeted costs for each task and the sum of these is the budget for the total project. The budget should show the anticipated level of expenditure at any given point in the project's schedule. This is termed the Budgeted Cost of the Work Schedule (BCWS). It is the product of the budget cost and the planned percentage completion, expressed as a fraction.

It is a fact of project life that percentage completion rarely equates to what was scheduled. Obtaining an estimate of the percentage completion for a task, and multiplying it by the budget cost, results in a new measure — the Budgeted Cost of the Work Performed (BCWP). This is the project's earned value at the point of measurement. If BCWP is less than BCWS, then the project is behind schedule.

Of course it is unlikely that the earned value will be the same as the Actual Cost of the Work Performed (ACWP) and this gives another useful comparison. If ACWP is greater than BCWP then this would be an indicator that the project may go over budget. If it were lower it could indicate that, perhaps, insufficient resources were being allocated to the project.

The differences, or variances, mentioned provide two key monitoring measures for projects:

☛ Scheduled Variance (BCWP – BCWS)
☛ Cost Variance (BCWP – ACWP).

As indicated, earned value analysis is usually performed first on individual tasks and then totalled for all tasks to give the figures for the full project. Therefore, for those tasks that are completed at the time of the analysis, the Earned Value will equal the budget figure.

Number	Task Description	Budget Staff-hours	% Achieved	Earned Value	Actual Staff-hours
1 2 And so on to all tasks					
	Total Project	Total		Total	Total

One of the reasons for doing earned value calculations is to attempt to predict costs to completion. This is done by linear extrapolation of the numbers. However the technique does assume that the estimates were accurate in the first place. It also relies on a subjective judgement in many cases for percentage completion.

Exception Reporting

Most project information is analysed by variance — difference between planned and actual performance. In this sense, the project manager is principally interested in exceptions to planned performance (of course, management by exception has an application far beyond the boundaries of project management).

03-3

Variances can be positive, negative or neutral: it is up to the project manager to determine what is useful in analysing individual situations. Variance can be used in any control system, mechanical, electrical, etc. to provide feedback and correction. But the principle does not transfer without issue to the sphere of project management. Accuracy is compromised by human characteristics: selectivity and subjectivity in particular.

A positive variance in a schedule is one where the event, usually a milestone, is early by comparison with the plan. In the same way, a negative variance is one where the event or milestone is later than scheduled. However, a positive variance is not necessarily good news. It may mean that quality has been sacrificed or that shortcuts have been taken which could result in safety defects, or reduced reliability. There may have been extra effort, and hence extra cost involved — the implication is that variances need to be analysed in the round, taking in cost, time and quality assessments of the same activities.

PAUSE TO REFLECT

What drawbacks does the system of exception reporting have?

Now read on.

The principles behind exception reporting are derived from Drucker's theory of Management by Objectives (MBO). The essence of MBO is that the organization, its departments and its people should focus on the few activities and issues that are critical to business success — all else is commentary. Since the early 1970s when he first published them, Drucker's ideas have been applied widely in corporate and public sector organizations — we see them in time management programmes, and they are especially visible in exception reporting.

Two serious flaws in MBO are that:

☞ It relies on a first-time identification of what really matters to the organization (what if something critical is overlooked?)
☞ It denies space for individual creativity and spontaneity.

Similar criticisms are levelled at exception reporting. The project manager, having identified a variance, still has to decide whether it is a significant variance. The danger can be that:

☞ The focus shrinks to variances identified as significant, while other 'insignificant' variances may develop unnoticed
☞ Non-variant areas will not be examined at all (this assumes a level of trust in forecast figures which may not be justified).

In a culture of reporting by exception, the unwritten rule is not to stick out — some reporting team members tend to develop a knack of producing non-variant data over time, and if there is no requirement to produce supporting evidence of performance data, genuine problems may remain hidden until they are unsolvable. For instance, where tasks have been started but are not complete, it is common to ask for estimates of percentage completion. It is not unknown for these estimates to be 99% for a long time!

Some of these may appear carping criticisms of a system which can be effective in prioritizing remedial action on projects. But experience in many organizations suggests that exception reporting is not by itself a sufficiently comprehensive approach to monitoring and review — occasionally it may make sense to institute random sampling or full review processes.

Large Projects

A monitoring difficulty peculiar to larger projects is the lag that can occur between occurrence, reporting and remedial action. If it takes weeks for a report to reach the project manager, it may take months before corrective action takes effect.

Managers of large projects therefore need to pay early attention to defining 'leading measures' — indicators which will give an early warning of underlying problems. These will of course be specific to individual contexts, but some practical examples include:

- ☛ Current levels of re-work required
- ☛ Volumes of overtime hours
- ☛ Inactivity on critical tasks or packages.

03-3-6 Managing Change

03-3

Changes to projects are also referred to as variations. It is inevitable that in most projects there will be changes. Because of the disruptive effect of change it is necessary that changes are managed smoothly and their effects translated into amended plans and schedules. Change implies some effect on cost, sometimes a net saving but more often escalation. It will inevitably have an effect on the schedule, always disruptive.

Changes in the project at the 'initiate' or feasibility stage (some would say that feasibility is about examining changes) are usually inexpensive as almost the only costs involved are those of a few people. At the design or 'specify' stage, change tends to cost more but even at this stage they are not likely to be excessive, since the total project resource requirement will not yet have been identified, much less committed. During the first two project stages then, change is relatively easily managed — the only prospect to concern the project manager is the likelihood of delay.

Changes made after the design stage however are nearly always costly and disruptive.

They want three lanes in each direction!

Planning and Controlling Projects

Many companies apply a 'design freeze' on completion of the design. If manufacture has started, the cost in lost time and scrap material, if a significant change has to be introduced, can be enormous. This is the reason why so many project management practitioners, and contracting organizations, insist on the 'fly before buy' approach where nothing is left to chance before the go-ahead to build.

However, as we have seen, not all change can be ruled out — nearly all projects are prey to some uncertainty. One protective aid the project manager can employ is a system for managing change.

The process starts with an early warning system to detect problems and opportunities which might affect the project. These must be kept under review, with continuous assessment of their potential impact upon the project if translated into changes. Only changes which are beneficial or unavoidable should be adopted.

There are a number of areas from which change can come:

☞ *Design.* Modifications to improve the design may be suggested after work has started. Often these are seen as technical improvements and will come from the conceptual design area. The project manager should take a fairly tough-minded approach to these ideas, many of which will tend to be from the 'wouldn't it be nice if' school. Modifications to design suggested after implementation are likely to be enormously disruptive.

☞ *External Stakeholder.* There may be changes in the market for the product that mean the output or product specification must change.

☞ *Organizational.* There may be changes within a client or supplier company which will mean the project cannot remain as it is (a typical example would be where a client company is taken over: the new owner may not wish to continue the project in its present form, or at all).

☞ *Personnel.* Changes in personnel are likely to have a disruptive effect on the schedule, particularly where the outgoing individuals have held key positions within the project structure.

☞ *Regulatory.* For instance, a change in safety legislation may affect the construction of a site or the fabrication of a product.

☞ *Political.* Both local and national government, often influenced by pressure groups, can have direct and indirect impact on projects.

☞ *Environmental.* Should it be discovered that there are environmental issues associated with the project, it would be unwise in the current climate to ignore them.

In management of change, the potential impact of changes in a project are evaluated prior to deciding whether or not to go ahead. Particularly in large or complex projects, where a single change may start a domino cascade of other modifications, it is customary to institute a formal change request procedure.

www.universal-manager.co.uk

ACTIVITY 16

What do you think is the purpose of a change request procedure?

03-3

Compare your suggestions with ours in the commentary in Appendix 1.

Typical items of documentation within a change request procedure are:

(1)   A Change Register or Log
(2)   A Change Request Form, sometimes known as a Variation Request Form
(3)   A Change or Variation Authorization Form.

What follows is a description of how a typical procedure is implemented.

After a proposed change has been entered in the change register, an impact assessment should follow, to determine the cost and time implications of the change. If this shows that change is beneficial or necessary a change request form is completed. This will have a description section for the proposed change, a reason/benefits area, a part for the decision to be recorded and a comments section. There should also be guidance on authorization levels.

CHANGE REQUEST FORM

Originated by: _____ Date: _____
(Complete Change details section)

Action approved: _____ Date: _____
(T P Manager or Director)

Action by: Date by:
Publications Manager   YES/NO
Editor   YES/NO
Design Co-ordinator   YES/NO
Author   YES/NO
Sales/Marketing   YES/NO

Ref: (Title/Chapter/Page nos, etc. to be completed by Originator)

IMMEDIATE ACTION
Remove existing master from production YES/NO
Signed: _____ (Director)

Change details: (To be completed by Originator - Attach copy if necessary)

Cost estimates:

Schedule impact:

Action completed by:	Initials:	Date:	Action completed by:	Initials:	Date:
Publications Manager			Author		
Editor			Sales/Marketing		
Design Co-ordinator					

To Project Manager:

Changes completed. Issue MCRS and replacement masters.

Signed: _____ (T P Manager/Director)

Changes may be rejected, accepted for implementation, accepted subject to conditions or left to be carried out on completion of the project. Financial authorization will be needed for change. If the change involves a contractor or subcontractor then it is unlikely that competitive tenders can be obtained. There is no incentive for a low price to be quoted. In projects where the bidding is very competitive, contractors have been known to rely on change orders to make some profit!

After a change has been accepted a change authorization form is completed, with any conditions imposed on the change, allowing work to start. The final decision should be entered in the change register and the cost and schedule outlooks for the project should be updated.

03-3

Issues and Opportunities

An issue is something that has happened and that could adversely affect the project. An opportunity is something that might happen and, if it did, could benefit the project. Both have to be addressed and managed. The first has more urgency but the latter cannot be ignored, as the benefits are usually present throughout the life cycle of the project's end result.

Issues rarely just happen — most often there are detectable symptoms which the attentive project manager will identify early and use to come up with an appropriate diagnosis.

PAUSE TO REFLECT

What symptoms of emerging issues have you come across in your experience of projects?

Now read on.

Some examples of the observable symptoms of developing problem situations are:

- ☞ *Late delivery.* This may involve a key item of equipment that will prevent schedule progress on dependent activities downstream. Sometimes it may be a minor item in terms of cost but major in terms of its effect.
- ☞ *Requests for additions.* Changes to scope can have a disruptive effect on the schedule. A key question is, do these come from the client or members of the team?
- ☞ *Cost overrun.* It is critical to determine where the money is going. Is there some endemic reason for overspend that will continue during the project? If resources are on track, is the problem with expenses or overtime or are there personnel working on other tasks but booking time to the project?
- ☞ *Omissions from scope.* This can happen by oversight and can take the project by surprise. What happened to the checking procedures?
- ☞ *Deviation from specification.* Here the project manager will want to know when and how substandard performance was identified, what caused it and whether it is continuing.
- ☞ *Lack of resources.* Not enough resources to maintain the schedule. Were the resources promised and what is the reason for shortage? Who should have supplied them?
- ☞ *Lack of confidence from client.* This can lead to tension and perhaps a predisposition on the part of the client to get too closely involved, leading in turn to a cagey project manager and a demoralized team.
- ☞ *Team conflicts.* The consequences of these are obvious both to the schedule and the quality of work on the project.
- ☞ *Staff shortages.* The need to make good staff shortages may have budget implications if the shortage can be resolved with money, or schedule implications if it can't.
- ☞ *Resistance from other departments.* Internal company politics can seriously disrupt schedules and budgets.

A question that should always be asked in connection with some symptoms is why they were not noticed before and do they point to a fundamental problem in the way the project was set up?

Having identified threatening symptoms, there should be a clear procedure in place for dealing with them. A similar procedure may be followed to that already described for change requests. In effect, the process of identifying and managing issues or problems is the risk management process — again the sense of integrating risk management within total project management is underlined.

Opportunities

Opportunities are 'upside risks' to be exploited for the benefit of the project. At the start of a project, opportunities should be looked for so that they can be incorporated early into project (or risk management) plans, preferably at the feasibility stage. But clearly, many opportunities arrive at later stages, and the project should have a robust system for analysing their potential benefits and capitalizing on them where appropriate.

A typical area where an opportunity might occur is that of technology: key breakthroughs may be achieved while the project is active (of course they can equally threaten the validity of the project's specification or current use of technology). Changes in raw material prices, sources and specifications could represent opportunities. Some may involve major changes like siting a facility or redesigning to incorporate the properties of a new material. In a similar vein, the predicted demand for a product may have increased since project approval. This may simply call for greater resourcing, but equally, larger scale production might entail re-design.

03-3

03-4   EVALUATION

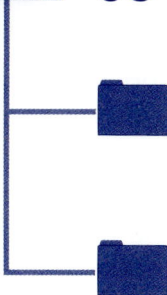

03-4

03-4 EVALUATION

Throughout a project there should be continuous evaluation at each stage. Typically the project cycle places 'gates' between each project stage — the permit to go through each gate is an evaluation that shows the project still on course to meet its objectives.   The nature and detail of evaluation can vary for each stage, and usually the 'specify' or feasibility stage requires the most rigorous evaluation. Get this wrong and a non-viable project may start to accumulate high costs or a valuable project may be lost.

At each stage there should be a financial evaluation — in fact finance is usually central to the decision on whether or not to proceed with a project, and financial evaluation methods are the most complex. For these reasons we will concentrate on financial evaluation methods in this section, although other evaluation methods will also be considered.

03-4-1 Financial Evaluation

The most important financial evaluation is the one carried out in the 'specify' or feasibility stage of a project, since its outcome will determine a go/no go decision on committing significant resources to the project. It can be problematic on some projects that key decisions have to be taken at early stages where least is known and where the data is least accurate.   Two alternative approaches to this problem are:

- Adopting the 'fly before buy' stance where samples or prototypes are developed before full commitment — that way the decision-maker has the closest thing to data on actual performance. In some industries a variation on this approach is 'phasing', where cost effective small-scale developments are expanded if the initial phase is successful.
- Obtaining data that is as accurate and up to date as possible in the circumstances, and covering deficiencies with a 'risk evaluation' — we will discuss this type of evaluation later in the section.

There are a number of methods for project evaluation; some are quick and approximate, while others are lengthy and detailed. Each has its particular area of application. The main ones are:

- Payback Time
- Return on Investment (ROI)
- Net Present Value (NPV)
- Discounted Cash Flow (DCF).

Payback Time

This is the time when positive cash flow generated by the project equals negative cash flow. It is very a simple technique and particularly suited to the 'initiate' stage of projects when information is only in outline, but is a good guide even at the 'specify' stage, and also very useful during any stage of a project when modification is suggested.

Payback time is calculated by:

$$\frac{\text{Cost of Modifications}}{\text{Annual Savings}} = \text{Payback Time}$$

Suitable payback time is of course specific to context: three to four years is normally good for a construction project undertaken by a large organization, whereas a small manufacturer is unlikely to be able to wait more than a year for payback.

Strictly, tax should be taken into account in any profit or net cash flow but because the method is quick and simple, tax is usually left out. To avoid confusion it is best to state when presenting calculations like this whether tax is incorporated.

Return on Investment (ROI)

We must be careful with the definition of this formula. It should allow for tax and may or may not include working capital, so, again, it is best to specify whether the figures are before or after tax and if working capital is included.

Like payback time, ROI is a non-discounting method which doesn't take long-term financial factors into account, and therefore the calculated figure should be treated as a guide only. It is mainly used at the initiate stage when only ballpark numbers are known.

The basic formula is:

$$\text{ROI} = \frac{\text{Net Income per Year}}{\text{Total Investment}}$$

If the net cash flow is different each year, it is common to take the cumulative cash flow over the life of the project, and divide by the number of years of operation to give an average net cash flow per year. Sometimes it is worked out for individual years to see how it varies from time to time.

Planning and Controlling Projects

Depreciation

Depreciation is not a cash flow method, and is not included in the discounted cash flow methods of project evaluation to be dealt with later. However ROI calculations sometimes include depreciation. Bookkeeping methods treat depreciation as a cost. The rationale is that in the positive cash flow or profit, some money has to be put aside for future resource replacement so all of the cash flow is not available to distribute as dividends. ROI worked out this way is more meaningful where there are shareholding interests.

Discounting

Money is said to have a time value since it can be put to productive use. It can earn interest in a bank. Capital can also be put to use to add value such that the original sum becomes more with time by investment in a project. It is therefore useful to compare the return on an investment in a project with the equivalent return when it is invested with compound interest. In this situation there are three factors to be considered in compounding.

- ☛ Initial values of money or resources, i.e. the assets. In the case of money this is referred to as the 'principal'
- ☛ The time factor over which use of assets is considered
- ☛ The rate at which assets gain value, referred to as the 'interest rate'.

The basic model assumes that the gain in value is constant with time and is expressed as a percentage of the value at the start of the time period. Time is usually considered to be one year but could be any time period i.e. month, quarter, week, day, etc. The interest is usually expressed in terms of an annual rate but it too can relate to any time period, i.e. 2% per month.

If   P = Starting sum or principal
     i = Interest rate over time period considered. (Although usually expressed as a percentage, this appears as a fraction in calculations.)
     n = Number of time periods considered, normally but not necessarily, years.
     S = Sum after n time periods.

Sometimes the interest rate is referred to as the discount rate.

For compound interest it is shown that $S = P (1+i)^n$

The Equivalence Concept

By investing an amount P at the start (year 0) for n years when the interest rate is i, we obtain an amount S. In other words, S after n years is equivalent to P at the start (if interest rates are i, of course). This consideration is important when investing money when the amount P is known and S is calculated.

$(1+i)^n$ is known as the 'compounding factor', used to calculate the future value. It is always greater than 1.

However when it comes to a company making an investment, such as a process plant, an oil refinery, a tanker, etc., then what the company tries to predict is how much money it will receive and spend in the future. In other words the company:

☛ Knows S, and
☛ Wants to be able to calculate what this is equivalent to today, i.e. at time 0.

This is known as the 'present value' of sum S. And since the investment will last for many years, these sums will relate to different values of n. Relating them all to the start reduces them to a common base.

The same formula is used, except that this time we will know S and want to calculate P.

03-4

Since if $S = P(1+i)^n$ then $P = S(1+i)^{-n}$

$(1+i)^{-n}$ is known as the 'discounting factor', used to calculate the present value of sum S. When all of the present values are added together we get the 'net present value'. Tables of discount factors are published but it is easy to derive these, if required, from the basic formula. These are always less than unity.

ACTIVITY 17

Calculate the discount factor for nine years if the interest rate is 12%. Remember in the formula that the interest rate must be fractional.

Compare your answer with ours in the commentary in Appendix 1.

Planning and Controlling Projects

Cash Flow

This is the flow of cash into and out of a company and therefore it is important for the above reasons that over the life of a project, cash flow is positive. Cash flow concerns 'real' movements of money.

Financial or project evaluation is based on the measurement and summation of incremental cash flows throughout the life of the project.

We have already seen that a sum of money has to be related to time in order for its real value to be established. Therefore any discussions of cash flow must relate these to the time over which the flow takes place.

In any project money is spent from the beginning, rising to the highest values during the 'implement' stage.

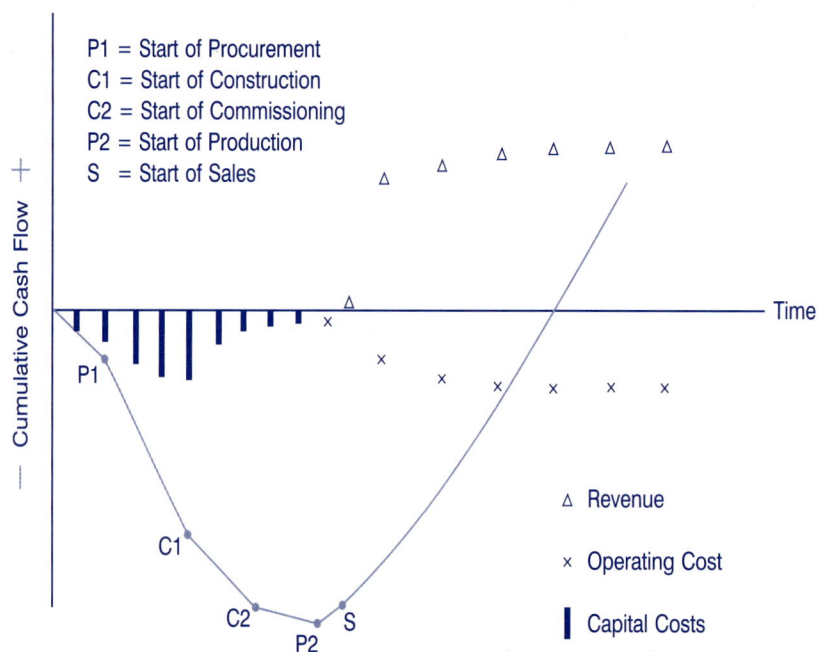

The illustration above shows cash flow over part of a project broken down into five stages which would typically occur on a construction project after design has been signed off:

- Procurement — purchase of equipment and material
- Construction
- Commissioning — testing and putting into operation of the construction
- Production — cost of operation, e.g. raw materials, labour, etc.
- Sale of product — the only source of positive cashflow.

108

Expenditure is highest in the first two 'sub-stages' and slows down during 'commissioning'. These are all negative cash flows over time. In the production sub-stage there will be fixed and variable costs which also constitute a negative cash flow. But the start of production is also the point at which income or revenue begins to be generated and the project experiences its first positive cash flow which, it is to be hoped, will outstrip negative cashflow at an early point in the sales sub-stage.

There is an important detail in the cost of production which we have not yet considered. In manufacturing costs and those costs used in cash flow calculations *depreciation is not a cash flow*. It is an accounting method for recovering the money spent on capital assets. The cash flow associated with the capital investment occurs at the start of the project where it is a negative cash flow. Cash flow is associated with actual flow of cash and the time at which it takes place.

However depreciation does have a secondary effect on the cash flow calculation. Depreciation affects the tax that is paid on profits, and this **is** an actual flow of cash. The government allows depreciation to be treated as an operating expense in the calculation of profit. Tax is calculated on the profit and has to be paid. Tax is therefore a negative cash flow and should be part of the cash flow calculation.

03-4

Cash flows mentioned so far have been mainly negative. The most obvious source of positive cash flow is sale of products, but where a project will not produce a saleable product, positive cashflow may derive from:

☞ Stage payments from the sponsor (in this case, a negative cash flow analysis may be needed to calculate optimum timing of stage payments)
☞ Grants or loans from the sponsor (or even stakeholders)
☞ Savings in operational costs
☞ Sale of equipment or materials at the end of a project.

Net cash flow in any period is the difference between the positive and negative cash flows.

Truly accurate cash flows can only be obtained after the money has been spent, i.e. at the end of the project. However project evaluation is an attempt to predict the future. Cash flows are therefore predictions that are based on the best information available. If, at a later date, these can be compared with actual flows, this will yield valuable historical information which should be stored within the organizational 'knowledge bank' to be referred to when planning similar projects in future.

Spend Curve

Capital expenditure usually occurs over a comparatively short period in relation to the life of the total project. The diagram drawn to show expenditure over time is usually known as the 'spend curve' — it tends to take the classical S-shape. Initial expenditure is slow, then builds up steeply, slowing down again in the final stages of the project. The ideal curve is continuously plotted against time but it is often more practical to plot the quantities at discrete but short time intervals.

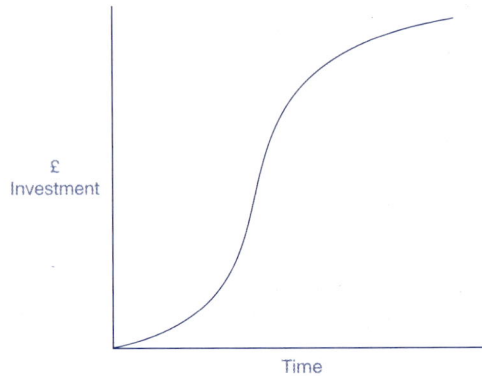

A predicted spend curve is a common requirement for project evaluation. It should include all expenditure from design right through to the commissioning (over-simplified project evaluations often assume that all capital expenditure occurs at the start, i.e. time zero.)

Cumulative Cash Flow Diagram

Another useful tool in project evaluation is a plot of the predicted cumulative cash flow with project time which can identify (among other things) the time when the cumulative cash flow is zero (effectively the break-even point).

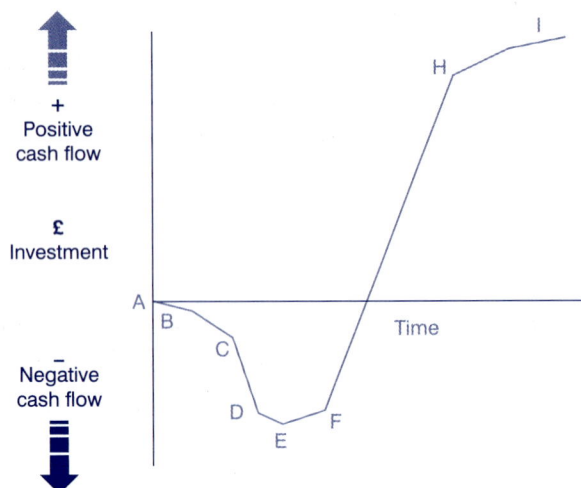

www.universal-manager.co.uk

Our illustration shows a typical cumulative cashflow diagram for a construction project to build a manufacturing plant:

AB The 'initiate' phase. This is to determine if the project is viable and to select the alternatives. The costs here are small and include the costs of carrying out the project evaluation itself.

BC The 'specify' phase. The expenditure and rate of expenditure is greater than previously as more personnel are drawn in, but it would still be modest compared to later phases. Point B is the usual start of the expenditure for project evaluation purposes since AB costs are often 'sunk costs' — paid for out of company overheads.

CD This is the period of rapid expenditure when major equipment is being bought, followed by expensive civil and construction work. Large numbers of people are being employed.

DE Here the construction work has all but finished and the plant is being commissioned. The number of people employed has dropped considerably.

EF At point E the plant has started to make saleable product. There may still be some expenses associated with construction/commissioning.

FG The plant is now in normal production mode and point G is where the total income is equal to the total expenditure. This is the 'break-even point' — sometimes used to give a quick measure of project viability.

GH Continued positive cash flow.

HI The plant is reaching the end of its economic life and the net cash flow may reduce owing to factors like greater maintenance costs, price reductions, etc.

I The end of the total project life cycle. There may be a cash flow associated with sale of the plant, but more than likely the scrap value will be balanced by the dismantling and removal cost.

03-4

Net Present Value

This method is also termed NPV, 'Present Value' and 'Present Worth'. All cash flows are related back to the present using discount factors. The sum of the cash flows, after each has been discounted back to the present, are then added. This gives the NPV.

The discount rate used is the one relevant to the circumstances (sometimes referred to as the minimum attractive rate of return — MARR). No company would want to invest for less than the money it would earn in an investment account — a greater return would be expected because of the higher risks almost certainly inherent in undertaking a project.

Computer spreadsheets are ideal for NPV and discounting calculations — current software will have the required formulae built in.

For an investment to be attractive it must have an NPV greater than 0. A negative NPV would mean that the investment did not meet the criteria set. What follows is a worked example.

CASE STUDY

A manufacturer is investing in new equipment. At the start £175,000 is spent, followed by a further £125,000 at the end of the first year. The equipment will have a salvage value of £50,000 by the end of the sixth year. The net cash flows are expected to be:

Period	2	3	4	5	6
Net Cash Flow £ '000	30	75	75	100	100

If the discount rate is 15%, what is the Net Present Value?

Year	Cash Flow	Discount Factors	Present value
0	− 175	1.000	− 175.00
1	− 125	0.870	− 108.75
2	30	0.756	22.68
3	75	0.658	49.35
4	75	0.512	38.40
5	100	0.497	49.70
6	150	0.432	64.80
		NPV =	− 58.82

This would be an unacceptable investment when funds are worth 15%. The minimum acceptable solution is zero NPV as this would mean a balance with the cost of funds.

Total Projects

Total projects are worked out in tabular form — usually on a spreadsheets package. The layout may plot expenditure in columns against time periods in rows, or vice versa.

	Year	0	1	2						n
1	Capital Cost									
2	Grant									
3	Working Capital									
4	Sales Revenue									
5	Production Cost									
6	Net Operating Cash Flow									
7	Capital Cost – Grant									
8	Depreciation for Tax									
9	Taxable Profit									
10	Tax Payable									
11	After Tax Operating Cash Flow									
12	Net Cash Flow									
13	Discount Factor									
14	Present Value									
	NET PRESENT VALUE									

Notes
2.   For capital cost in Year 1, the grant (say 20% of capital) would go into Year 2.
3.   Working capital is not normally included in grant or depreciation. It is assumed that it can be fully recovered by the end of the project. (Working capital includes stocks, spares, etc.)
8.   This is whatever percentage of 'capital cost – grant' is allowed by the Tax Authorities.
9.   This is 6 – 8.
10.   This is tax (Corporation Tax) calculated on 9, but is entered in following year.
11.   This is 6 – 10.
12.   This is 1 + 2 + 3 (which are negative) + 11
14.   This is 13 x 12.

Net Present Value is the sum of all the Present Values from year 1 to Year n in row 14.

03-4

Discounted Cash Flow

Also termed DCF or 'Internal Rate of Return' (IRR), this value is obtained by using a range of discount factors in the NPV calculation already described and obtaining the one that gives a zero NPV. In our case study example, there was a negative NPV for a discount rate of 15%. However there is a calculable interest rate which gives a zero NPV. This is the internal rate of return for the project — IRR.

A DCF calculation is one where the discount rate that gives NPV = 0 is found. This, if done manually, is unfortunately a trial and error calculation. We continue our case study below.

CASE STUDY

Year	Factor 12%	Present Value	Factor 10%	Present Value
0	1.000	− 175.00	1.000	− 175.00
1	0.893	− 111.63	0.909	− 113.63
2	0.797	23.91	0.826	24.78
3	0.712	53.40	0.751	56.33
4	0.636	47.70	0.683	51.23
5	0.567	56.70	0.621	62.1
6	0.507	75.05	0.564	84.60
NPV		− 29.87		− 9.56

By extrapolation (i.e. the %age that would give zero) the IRR is 9%.

Projects usually have a minimum IRR below which the client/sponsor is not interested in investing.

www.universal-manager.co.uk

ACTIVITY 18

Explain the differences between Payback Time, Net Present Value, and DCF Return on investment for assessing the viability of projects.

03-4

Compare your answers with our suggestions in the commentary in Appendix 1.

Refining Financial Evaluation

As a project progresses, initial financial calculations will need to be refined, particularly for commercial ventures where increasingly accurate projections will be required for revenue generation. More accurate data should also be available for the calculation of operating and maintenance costs.

The Payback, ROI, NPV and IRR calculations should be repeated to ensure the project is still viable, and to assess the effect of design and planning definitions on project finance. In the 'specify' stage, financial evaluation will be looking at cost detail to ensure that the figures are at least in line with earlier predictions. In the 'implement' phase the focus will be on continuous comparison of the achieved expenditure against budget (derived from the cost estimate produced during project planning).

03-4-2   Other Types of Evaluation

Although financial evaluation tends to take precedence on most projects, there are various other kinds of evaluation which can contribute to an assessment of project viability, progress and success. Many of these rely on qualitative data to some extent, which in itself may provide a large clue as to why many organizations prefer to rely on financial indicators.

Technical Evaluation

Where there are alternative technologies to achieve the same end, these have to be evaluated to select the optimum technology. It is common to tie technical evaluation in with the financial assessment since technology is often a significant expenditure item. For instance, a common situation is where one technology is low on capital cost but high on operating cost and the other high in capital, but low on operating (the same considerations come into play when deciding whether to buy or lease equipment).

Alternative technologies will be therefore be considered primarily from a financial standpoint, but other significant factors must also be looked at under the headings:

☞ Operations
☞ Fit
☞ Risk.

PAUSE TO REFLECT

What questions might be raised about alternative technologies under these three headings?

Now read on.

The project manager would want to be assured that any equipment (and materials) selected will be capable of competent use by the project team or by specialists, without incurring undue costs (on training or sub-contracting). He must be convinced that the technology will produce the required results, and that it will be compatible with systems or tools already in use. It is crucial to take into account the maintenance and upgrade requirement for any new equipment, and to assess the risk of obsolescence. Some of these criteria are subjective, and it is often an effective tactic to involve the 'users' in decision-making before new technology is selected — this may involve a trial before a full commitment is made.

Operational Assessment

This assessment looks at the factors that affect project operation:

☞ Are the right people available?
☞ Do they have the correct mix of skills or will they need training?
☞ Is the required infrastructure in place to support the operation? This will include the physical infrastructure, the communications system and the organizational structure.
☞ Can the materials required be obtained and made available in time and in the correct form?
☞ Are support services available? This will range from accounting and legal services through to utilities such as electricity, water and fuel.

Operational assessment is in fact a check on the effectiveness of project definition and planning which should have covered all of these matters — in that sense it is an aspect of risk assessment.

Economic Assessment

Economic evaluation is not about money but relates to resources and the wider community: how these will be affected by the project and what impact will they have in turn? Economic assessment too may be considered part of the risk management process.

An exhaustive survey of economic factors and their influence is perhaps not a realistic aim (except for very large, or very high profile undertakings) but, by checklist or brainstorm, the project team should be able to identify the chief economic factors and identify their likely interaction with the project.

The assessment should be performed by those familiar with economic factors such as:

- ☛ Effects of/on local employment
- ☛ Impact of/on the local community
- ☛ Impact of/on property or land values
- ☛ Impact of/on local infrastructure, particularly where developments are in train.

Clearly, smaller projects are more likely to be affected *by*, than to have an effect *upon* these spheres. Larger projects may budget for local consultants to carry out their economic assessment.

Environmental Assessment

Many projects will have an effect on the environment, especially those involving extraction, construction or manufacture. It is now a requirement in most industrial projects to prepare an assessment of environmental impact, and to develop measures for minimizing disruption, displacement or damage within the vicinity affected by the project.

Environmental assessments also require specialist skills and knowledge to be undertaken.   The assessor will need to gauge the likely impact on:

- ☛ Local residents
- ☛ Plant and animal life
- ☛ Land, air and water qualities
- ☛ Noise levels
- ☛ Aesthetic appearance.

Numerous large projects (particularly in the petrochemical and nuclear fuel sectors) have faltered owing to their failure to predict environmental impact and to assuage the hostility of local residents and 'green' pressure groups.

Impact Assessment

This type of evaluation attempts to identify **all** factors which may affect a project, and to determine their likely impact — in other words, impact assessment is a composite of all the evaluation methods we have described so far (and is a component of risk management).

Various impact assessment models have been developed and refined since the 1970s. The most comprehensive will probe prevailing and predicted conditions in the following areas:

- Society
- Technology
- Economics
- Environment
- Politics.

ACTION ACTIVITY 19

You may already be familiar with the STEEP model (or with the associated STEP, PEST and PESTLE models). For this Activity you should:

- Identify an impact assessment model with relevance to a project or programme with which you are involved
- Find out how to apply the model
- Apply your chosen model and record your findings.

The internet is a helpful source of information on this subject. One site we can recommend as a starting point is:

www.focusintl.com/strategy

Now read on.

Risk Assessment

In Dossier 02 *Delivering Successful Projects* we describe the current approach to risk management in projects which is to integrate risk analysis and contingency planning within the mainstream of project management. For operations where, for whatever reason, total risk management is not in place, risk assessment is often relied upon as the chief method for identifying and controlling the uncertainty inherent within projects.

In the light of current knowledge and experience about why projects succeed or fail, this bolt-on approach is not recommended. Isolated risk assessment may well identify all the sources of uncertainty within (and without) a project, but the process is unlikely to be sufficiently embedded to ensure that:

☞   Alternative strategies for dealing with risk are agreed
☞   Project plans are continuously refined as the rolling risk management programme evolves.

These are two key deliverables of a risk management strategy designed to ensure that all project personnel are aware of project risks and how to handle them, and that risk is minimized throughout the life of the project.

To be sure, the greatest uncertainty will be at the start of a project, and this is also the best time to put measures in place to minimize risk — the further a project proceeds, the greater the cost of making changes.

Right at the outset, one of the major sources of risk is in taking a decision between alternative projects or alternative approaches to achievement of the same strategic objective. The best option, after evaluating several, is usually subjected to a sensitivity analysis based on quantitative calculations. These are predominantly financial, but can also take in factors such as market segmentation and resource capacity. Alternative approaches are interrogated by feeding in variations to key aspects of the outline project plan (such as equipment purchase, labour costs or overall timing).

Post-project Evaluation

One of the most important evaluations an organization should make occurs at the end of a project. This is the post-mortem after completion or handover. The focus here should be on learning lessons for the future, since actual project performance cannot be affected. An effective post-project evaluation should form part of the project's closure, and is discussed in Dossier 02 of *The Universal Manager* series — *Delivering Successful Projects*.

APPENDIX 1

COMMENTARY ON ACTIVITIES

Activity 2

In general terms the four required components are defined as follows:

- *Intention.* It must be stated that both parties to a contract intend it to be legally binding.
- *Offer and acceptance.* The client must make a definite offer, specifying terms, and the contractor must explicitly accept the offer. This is an essential aspect of a project — the specific terms ('the specification') must be clear and agreed — any room for dispute may rebound on the client, contractor or both at a later stage
- *Consideration.* This means that each side must promise something of value to the other: this promise is usually insured by contract clauses defining what will constitute a breach of contract
- *Capacity.* This requires the client to ensure that it can fulfil the offer to the contractor (of payment) — if the client does not have the capacity to meet its side of the bargain, the contract can be declared void.

Activity 4

Here are some brief definitions of a range of standard contract clauses:

Limits of liability
Limits the liability of either party for costs not covered by insurance. Usually these are for costs resulting from failure to meet some of the guarantees on delivery, performance or mechanical integrity. A definition that limits the maximum loss is required. It is usually a clause for negotiation. Contractors prefer this to be less than the profit on the job — the buyer prefers it to be as high as possible to provide an incentive and concentrate the mind of the supplier.

Payment terms
The way in which money flows from purchaser to contractor is critical. The contractor will want the job to be self-financing whereas the purchaser wants to pay for work done. To prevent financial problems, the payment terms need to be defined precisely.

Variations or changes to contract

Very often, the purchaser will wish to make changes (perhaps to the specification) after the contract has started. These can be extremely expensive due to their disruptive effect. The way in which such changes will be handled and costed must be defined in the contract. On competitive jobs, variations sometimes represent one of the few opportunities for the contractor to make a profit. The purchaser, when drawing up a contract, should be aware of the high cost of 'change orders'. Conditions under which **cost escalation** will be acceptable, and the process for obtaining approval for payments based on escalated costs, should be defined in a similar fashion.

Force majeure

These are factors over which the contractor has no control and which can be reasons for non-performance of contract. The clear cut ones are those that are often defined as 'Acts of God, fires, earthquakes, flood, tempest, hostilities, war, invasion, civil disorder, etc.'. Force majeure applies to circumstances beyond the reasonable control of either party. One difficult area is the incidence of strikes and industrial action. Many purchasers will contend that these are at least partly within the control of the contractor.

Performance tests

The conditions for tests on the contractor's performance or output need to be tightly defined since the results will largely determine whether the project has been carried out to an acceptable standard. This in turn will affect the final payment made to the contractor.

Insurance and risk

There will be a number of requirements for insurance, especially if there is construction or other high risk work in the contract. The contractor is obliged to repair all damage for which he is responsible, and in the case of death or injury to indemnify the purchaser if it occurred as a result of the contractor's action, negligence, or breach of statutory duty. It must be clear who is responsible for arranging insurance.

Sub-contractors

All large contracts involve sub-contractors. Clients often wish to reserve the right to approve any sub-contractors and ensure that the conditions of the main contract extend to them. There will also be a clause stating that the contractor is not allowed to assign (transfer the benefits of the contract) to another party not named in the contract without the permission in writing of the purchaser.

Suspension and termination

The conditions under which the contract can be suspended (put in abeyance) or terminated (permanently suspended) need to be anticipated and defined. In particular the financial arrangements need to be made clear.

Performance bond

A client who is obliged to complete the payments before the project's outputs have been fully tested will need some protection should the product or service not meet its performance specification. The performance bond is a guarantee given by a bank or insurance company. The amount, period of validity, procedure for forfeiture and arrangements for release of money need to be specified.

Arbitration

In the event of a dispute that cannot be resolved by discussion, it is usual in contracts to make provision for arbitration. The contract should nominate the Arbitrator whose judgement will be defined as either binding or non binding. 'Binding' means the parties agree to abide by the arbitrator's judgement, 'non binding' means that the parties are still free to go to court.

Confidentiality

Both parties will usually agree to keep specified information confidential unless it is already in the public domain.

Purchaser's obligations

This will detail the equipment, materials, information, etc. that the client is bound to provide to the contractor.

Contractor's obligations

This clause will deal with factors affecting time and the quality of project outputs. Often covered here are: the design work to be carried out by the contractor; standards for drawings and documentation; and the conditions to be observed by the contractor when on the client's site.

Intellectual property

Intellectual property is defined in law as any recorded result of the thought process or intellect. Typical examples are inventions, designs, art and literature. Many organizations now treat intellectual property as an asset, and some go as far as accounting for it. Where a project will generate new ideas, designs, processes or literary works it is usual for the contract to specify who has ownership of the intellectual product. This is an area of law which is fraught with complexity and various different arrangements and legislative references are possible. The main areas of legislation which may apply here include: patents, trademarks, registered designs, copyright and design right.

Activity 7

Some typical cost items are:

- ☞ *Labour.* An essential part of an estimate is the number of hours for each type of professional, craft or manual labour. These will be from in-house data sources and will normally be given as hourly rates including employee on-costs and overheads. Certain parts of a project, such as design, may be sub-contracted and a quote for a lump sum price, against a specification of requirements, would be sought.

- ☞ *Materials.* Unit costs are often obtained from suppliers' price lists, even for industry-specific items like concrete, brick, steel sections, cables, wiring, piping, etc. The accuracy of the final estimate will depend heavily on accurate estimation of quantities. Ideally, buyers will be authorized to pool resources and negotiate for discounts and this should be taken into account during estimating.

- ☞ *Equipment.* Prices of smaller mass produced items can be from manufacturers' price lists. Cost savings are possible by shopping around. Some equipment items are large one-off purchases (e.g. a main frame computer built to the client's specification). The important thing here is to specify exactly who supplies what. If, say, the project requires a large 10MW compressor, do you want the supplier to provide the electric motor to drive it? If not, who takes responsibility if the compressor plus motor doesn't operate as required?

- ☞ *Sub-contracted work.* A price for sub-contracted work should be agreed before preparation of a detailed estimate by the sub-contractor against a specification. The specification must be as detailed and complete as possible to avoid later variations to contract.

- ☞ *Overheads.* The costs described above have all been 'direct costs'. That is, they can be directly attributed to the project. Overheads (or 'indirect costs') are not directly attributable to the project — they will tend to be costs associated with running the whole business, not just the project. Rent, heat, lighting and salaries for support staff are typical examples. Different companies will have different ways of dealing with overheads. Typical methods are to calculate them as percentages of the direct cost, or to base them on an hourly rate for labour. In fact most companies will use a mixture of methods. The figures and percentages will be derived from forecast business and will be designed to recover all the overheads.

- ☞ *Construction.* Many large projects have a construction phase. This will require the consumption of services such as fuel and electricity and consumables such as welding rods, paint, etc. There will be labour and management costs, travel and subsistence.

- ☞ *Commissioning.* Large or complex projects tend to have a testing and proving stage before project completion and handover. If it is a manufacturing plant or a process plant it will require the consumption of raw material as well as services like fuel, water and electricity. There will again be labour and management costs, travel and subsistence.

☞ *Inflation.* Any project lasting for more than a year should take this into account. Even in times of low inflation this could make for a significant increase on costs.

☞ *Currency.* Transnational projects may involve purchase of materials and equipment in different currencies. Fluctuation in exchange rates will affect the final cost.

☞ *Contingency.* There will always be some error in an estimate — the estimator's skill is in keeping these to a minimum. To allow for error, it is common practice to allow for contingency costs. The magnitude of this should ideally be based on past experience of similar projects.

Activity 9

With complex projects, the Gantt chart is not an effective medium for displaying the relationships of dependency and precedence. Our simple example might be easily amended (by means of connecting lines and arrows) to show these relationships — but as activities begin to multiply, the less clear these links become.

Furthermore, the chart does not show the requirement for or deployment of manpower resources. In our example, the activity times assume that people are available to complete the activity on time, but of course activity times can be shortened or lengthened by increasing or decreasing the resource allocation.

Activity 11

(a)   Choose the longest activity on the critical path (A, B, D, F, G, H) — which is G — and reduce to 4 weeks. Working through the diagram gives the new finish time of 22 weeks. When we redo the diagram we will see that there is a new and parallel critical path (A, B, D, I, J).

(b)   To get to 20 weeks we need to reduce both critical paths by 2 weeks. We could consider using the defined method of selecting the longest activity on the new critical path, e.g. I. However, logic tells us that if we consider those parts of the critical path that are common to both, only one reduction will be needed. Reducing activity B or D (let's say D) by 2 will give a finishing time of 20 weeks.

Note that path A, C, E, H, K now becomes critical. All paths are critical.

(c)   To reduce to 18 weeks, and still follow the rules, we could reduce each of B and C by 2 weeks.

(d)   The total reductions made are: G = 4, D = 2, B = 2 and C = 2, a total of 10 weeks, equal to £100,000.

Activity 12

In the version shown below, we have considered each activity starting as early as possible and have not shown floats for non-critical activities on the Gantt chart. This exercise can obviously be re-worked with activities starting as late as possible.

(a)

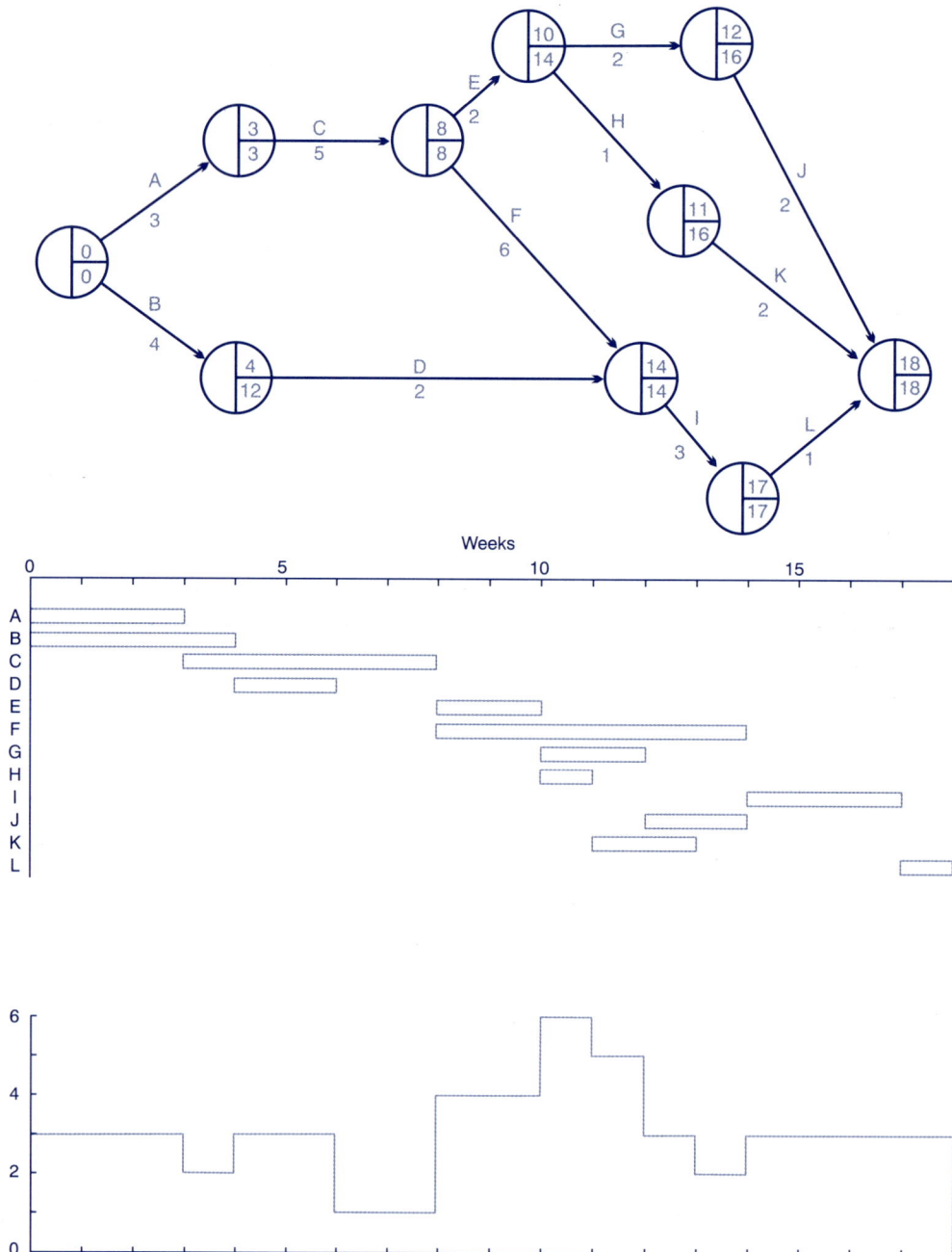

(b)   Total project time is 18 weeks
The critical path runs through A – C – F – I – L
The maximum resource required at any one time is 6 people
Week 11 is when resourcing is at maximum load.

Activity 13

The main issues here are to do with empowerment, sufficiency of information and confidentiality. In the main, it makes good sense for project team members to be informed not only of what is required of them, but also of the work being undertaken by the whole team. Seeing the critical path will enable team members to understand the interdependency of activities, and to appreciate critical areas. Giving them sight of budgetary information may form part of a policy of devolving budgetary responsibility, and impressing upon team members, the targets and forecast pattern for expenditure.

However, effective counter-arguments might be that:

☞ Many team members are external to the project managing organization and should not be party to restricted financial information
☞ The project is so large and complex that full critical path and budgetary information would be burdensome to the rest of the team.

Activity 16

An effective change request procedure fulfils several functions. Perhaps the key one is to ensure that any proposed change has been fully appraised. The following questions need to be asked:

☞ Is the change possible?
☞ Is it necessary?
☞ Who initiated it, client or contractor?
☞ What effect will it have on the programme?
☞ What is the estimated cost?
☞ Who will pay?
☞ Are there any safety, reliability or environmental implications?
☞ When should it be introduced?
☞ What will be the knock-on effects?

The procedure thus ensures a rigorous interrogation of any planned change, and a formal authorization.

Activity 17

$$(1+0.12)^{-9} = 0.3606$$

£100 received in 9 years' time at a discount rate of 12% would be worth 0.3606 x £100 = £36.06 today if the discount value is 12%.

Activity 18

Pay-Back Time is the time when the positive actual cash in flow equals the negative actual cash.

Net Present Value is the sum of the cash flows after each has been discounted back to the present.

DCF Return on Investment is the value of the discount factor that gives a zero Net Present Value.

APPENDIX 2

GLOSSARY

Change Control
Registering all potential modifications to the project; analysing their potential impact; and comprehensively identifying the consequences of any change. Also known as Variation Control.

Close Out
Completion of work once the project has been implemented.

Communication
Effective transmission and receipt of information in all available formats and media.

Configuration Management
An extension of Change Control, focussing on control of the technical configuration of a project.

Conflict Management
The art of managing conflict creatively.

Control and Co-ordination
Establishing targets, measuring actual performance, establishing variance and instituting necessary corrective action. Ensuring coherence and 'fit' between the work of various project participants, in line with overall project objectives.

Cost Control
The discipline of reconciling planned and actual money or time figures to physical parts of the project.

Delegation
The practice of getting others to perform work effectively which one chooses not to do oneself.

Estimating
Making a quantified assessment of the resources required to implement part or all of a project.

Finance
In a project context, finance is essentially the process of raising and managing the allocation of funds.

Industrial Relations
Management of the workforce, including, but not limited to, statutory responsibilities and duties, negotiating terms and conditions of pay and employment, union and non-union relations, and manpower planning.

Information Communication Technology (ICT)
Collective term for all automated systems used to transmit data: includes mobile telephones, the Internet, e-mail, video conferencing, digital television, etc.

Information Technology (IT)
Usually computer based technology for the collection, storage, processing and presentation of data.

Integration
Co-ordinating and controlling people, resources, processes and functions which may be dispersed geographically, functionally, temporally or hierarchically.

Law
The legal duties, rights and processes which govern in a project situation. There are several different categories of law. The most important include national legal systems, such as the criminal law, but particularly company and commercial law, employment laws, contract law, health and safety and other regulatory requirements such as planning law, data protection, sexual and racial discrimination building regulations, etc.

Leadership
Organizing, planning, controlling and directing resources. Motivating the project team.

Management Accounting
Allocating costs correctly to provide a clear view of current and forecast financial performance.

Marketing and Sales
Matching the capacity of an organization with the needs/desires of its client base to bring about the maximum possible advantage for both parties, then getting someone to buy the product or service being offered by the company.

Management Development
Staff planning, recruitment, development, training and assessment.

Mobilization
The initiation of project work typically involves bringing together project personnel and securing equipment and facilities. The term 'Project Start-Up' is often used to cover the same period.

www.universal-manager.co.uk

Negotiation
Attempting to achieve your own desired outcome from a transaction, while leaving all other parties equally satisfied at the subsequent outcome.

Operations and Technical Management
Management of the physical resources (usually labour, equipment and materials) required for design and production of a product or service.

Organization Design
Design of the most appropriate organizational structure for a project.

Performance Measurement
Measurement of a project's progress in relation to planned cost and schedule, sometimes using the calculation of Earned Value.

Planning
Creation of a project plan which details the project purpose, objectives, strategy, standards, key players, task breakdown, resource allocation, schedule and milestones.

Portfolio
A group of projects managed by the same organization, team or individual, which are not necessarily aligned towards the same strategic objective.

Post Project Appraisal
Usually carried out once a project's outputs or end results are in use. Chief purpose is to provide feedback in order to identify key lessons learned which can benefit future projects.

Procurement
Can include: an investment appraisal of the options available; procurement or acquisition strategy; preparation of contract documentation; acquisition; selection of suppliers; administration of contracts; and storage, inspection, expediting and handling of materials and equipment.

Programme
A group of projects which together contribute to the achievement of the same strategic objective.

Programme Management
Management of a suite of strategically aligned projects.

Project
A non-routine piece of work undertaken to deliver:
- A beneficial result
- Of a specified quality
- Within defined time and cost constraints
- And which contains an element of risk.

Project Appraisal
Calculating the viability of the project — will include financial, environmental, health & safety and performance appraisals.

Project Environment
All external influences which may be brought to bear on a project.

Project Life Cycle
The sequence of phases through which a project will pass from conception to completion.

Project Management
Planning, organization, monitoring and control of all aspects of a project, plus the motivation of all involved to achieve the project objectives safely and within agreed time, cost and performance criteria.

Project Strategy
High level, comprehensive definition of how a project will be developed and managed.

Project Success/Failure Criteria
APM identifies three different types of criteria:
- Those of the project sponsor or client
- Time, budget, and specification.
- Profitability.

Quality
Assuring that required standards of performance are attained. Includes: defining a Quality policy; establishing a system for Quality management; Quality Assurance (QA) which defines procedural and documentation requirements; and Quality Control (QC) — the process of measuring whether a pre-defined level of performance has indeed been achieved.

Risk Analysis and Measurement
Risk Management is the process of identification, assessment, analysis and management of all project risks.

Safety
Determining standards and methods to minimize the likelihood of accident or damage to people and equipment. Ensuring that these standards are respected in operation, and reviewing them to ensure their continued validity.

Scheduling
Selecting and applying the most appropriate techniques to create a timetable for delivery of project outputs on time and to specification.

Sub-project
A work package for which responsibility has been delegated to someone other than the leader of the overall project.

Systems and Procedures
These detail the standard methods, practices and processes for handling frequently occurring events within the project.

Systems Management
Prime activities are Systems Analysis, Systems Design and Engineering and Systems Development.

Team Building
Assembling the right project team, and creating a co-operative environment.

Value Analysis
Application of a similar series of techniques to an existing product, process or organization.

Value Engineering
Application of a series of proven techniques during the concept and design stages of a project.

Value Management
A structured means of improving business effectiveness in line with strategic goals: may incorporate techniques such as Value Engineering and Value Analysis.

Work Definition
The definition of project work and organization is achieved through the use of a Work Breakdown Structure (WBS) and an Organization Breakdown Structure (OBS).

Work Package
A component of the project: a piece of work contributing to project objectives, and which may be coupled with other work packages.

APPENDIX 3

USEFUL RESOURCES

W H Aitken (1997/98), *Project Management & Operations Research*, South Bank University London.

D H Allen (1991), *Economic Evaluation of Projects*, Institution of Chemical Engineers.

N M L Barnes (1990), *Financial Control*, Thomas telford Publications.

R Buttrick (1997), *The Project Workout*, Pitman Publishing.

J Chalmers (1997), *Managing Projects*, How To Books.

C Chapman & S Ward (1998), *Project Risk Management*, Wiley.

R K Corrie (1990), *Project Evaluation*, Thomas Telford Publications.

Project Magazine, produced by the Association for Project Management.

B Curtis, S Ward & G Chapman (1991), *Roles, Responsibilities and Risks in Management Contracting*, Construction Industry Research and Information Association.

M A Cusumano & K Nobeoka (1998), *Thinking Beyond Lean*, The Free Press.

S Ghoshal & C A Bartlett (1998), *The Individualized Corporation*, William Heinemann.

Publications.

R L Kliem & I S Ludin (1992), *The People Side of Project Management*, Gower.

B P Lientz & K P Rea (1998), *Project Management for the 21st Century*, Academic Press.

D Lock (1998), *Project Management*, Gower.

K Lockyer & J Gordon (1991), *Critical Path Analysis and Other Project Network Techniques*, Pitman.

P W G Morris (1997), *The Management of Projects*, Thomas Telford

G Reiss (1996), *Programme Management Demystified*, E & F N Spon.

J R Turner (1993), *The Handbook of Project-based Management*, McGraw-Hill.

C D J Waters (1989), *A Practical Introduction to Management Science*, Addison-Wesley.

WEBSITES

Association for Project Management
www.apm.org.uk
Project Management Resources
pmblvd.com
www.ccta.gov.uk/prince
www.pug.mcmail.com/pip/about-prince.html

APPENDIX 4

NEBS Management Diploma

NEBS Management is the Awarding Body for specialist management qualifications — committed to developing qualifications which meet the needs of today's managers at all levels across industry.

The NEBS Management Diploma is a broad management development programme aimed at practising and aspiring middle managers. It offers a comprehensive, integrated programme of personal and organizational development.

Content

During the Diploma programme, a candidate will:

☞ Establish a Personal Development Plan
☞ Study theory and practice in the following key management areas:
    ☞ Managing Human Resources
    ☞ Financial Management
    ☞ Organizational Activities and Change
    ☞ Management Skills
☞ Produce a specialist Management Report
☞ Compile an Individual Development Portfolio.

Flexibility

The NEBS Management Diploma requires a minimum of 240 hours of study but can be completed on a full-time or part-time basis as appropriate. Many programmes will offer a mix of direct training, open learning and practical work-based activity. In connection with the Universal Manager series, the Diploma therefore offers the facility for learning in a variety of media including paper-based material, on-line resources and taught elements.

Assessment

Assessment of performance takes a rounded view of the capability demonstrated by the candidate in assignments and specialist tasks, in the management report and portfolio, and in interview.

Enrolment

The usual entry requirements are:

- ☛ At least two years' relevant management experience
- ☛ PLUS a NEBS Management Certificate, a Management S/NVQ at Level 3 or the equivalent qualification.

There are many Accredited Centres approved to offer the Diploma programme in the UK and abroad. Call NEBS Management on **0171 294 3053** for details of your nearest Centre.

INDEX